DATE DUE

DEMCO 38-296

A Treasury of Business Quotations

A Treasury of
Business Quotations

by

Michael C. Thomsett

McFarland & Company, Inc., Publishers
Jefferson, North Carolina, and London

British Library Cataloguing-in-Publication data are available

Library of Congress Cataloguing-in-Publication Data

Thomsett, Michael C.
    A treasury of business quotations / by Michael C. Thomsett.
      p. cm.
    ISBN 0-89950-469-8 (lib. bdg. : 50# alk. paper) ∞
    1. Quotations, English. 2. Business—Quotations, maxims, etc.
3. Management—Quotations, maxims, etc. 4. Executive ability—
Quotations, maxims, etc. I. Title.
PN6084.B87T46 1990
082—dc20   89-27903
                                         CIP

Manufactured in the United States of America

McFarland & Company, Inc., Publishers
  Box 611, Jefferson, North Carolina 28640

Prologue

1 It is a good thing for an uneducated man to read books of quotations.
— Winston S. Churchill,
My Early Life, 1930, ch. 9

2 Be careful — with quotations you can damn anything.
— André Maurois,
address, Nov. 12, 1966

3 I hate quotations, tell me what you know.
— Ralph Waldo Emerson,
Journal, Dec. 20, 1822

4 People will accept your ideas more readily if you tell them Benjamin Franklin said it first.
— David H. Comins,
Washingtonian, Nov., 1978

Table of Contents

Table of Contents

Preface

Samuel Johnson, who is generously quoted in this book, said in the preface of his *Dictionary* (published in 1755), "I am not so lost in lexicography as to forget that words are the daughters of earth, and that things are the sons of heaven."

People involved in business, and the difficult issues they must confront on a daily basis, are the real and tangible subjects of this book. The words, by themselves, do not define business. It is the people and things that make a difference — in the business environment, the corporate culture, and the attitude of employees and employers as they confront their daily challenge.

The quotations selected for this work represent a number of subjects. Many present points of view that may be thought wise; others are of questionable wisdom. The business experts, philosophers, literary greats, and others quoted in these pages do have something to say to those in the business world, about management methods, human relations, or the often unspoken emotional side of the corporate culture. These thoughts may be expressed humorously, ironically, wisely, or poetically.

A quotation can be located in this collection in a number of ways: by general subject, by author, or by key word or phrase. Every quotation is numbered in sequence for easy cross-reference from the author and key word indexes at the back of the book.

Each quotation has been attributed as accurately as possible. Publication dates include months and days when possible; and chapter numbers or names are provided for quotations from books. Book references are not given by page number, since many books are published in different editions with different page numbering.

Quotations translated from other languages may vary from one source to another. When multiple translations were located, the one that seemed most clear or that best expressed the sentiment was used.

Modern-day business writers are sensitive to the reality that women are involved in business just as much as men. However, this has not always been the case. As an historical matter, quotations concerning business are markedly male oriented and no effort has been made to change this in the present compilation. I hope this work will prove to be a helpful reference in your business library.

The Treasury of Business Quotations

Ability

5 One good head is better than a hundred strong hands.
— Thomas Fuller, *Gnomologia*, 1732, no. 3753

6 Force has no place where there is need of skill.
— Herodotus, *The History*, ca. 450 B.C., book III, ch. 127

7 Most people don't manage to the utmost of their ability because they don't want to.
— Robert Heller, *The Super Managers*, 1984, ch. 1

8 I know of no more encouraging fact than the unquestionable ability of man to elevate his life by a conscious endeavor.
— Henry David Thoreau, *Walden,* 1854, 2, "Where I Lived and What I Lived For"

9 Nature has not endowed us all with the same powers

There are things that some of us cannot do.
— Aesop, fable, "Know Your Limitations," ca. 550 B.C.

10 We are not capable of everything.
— Virgil, *Eclogue,* VIII, ca. 25 B.C., line 63

11 One simple fact of life in organizations today is this: If competent people do not manage situations, then incompetent people will.
— William P. Anthony, *Managing Incompetence,* 1981, ch. 1

12 Competence always contains the seeds of incompetence.
— Laurence J. Peter, *Why Things Go Wrong,* 1985, ch. 2

13 One's ability to perform a given task competently decreases in proportion to the number of people watching.
— Mark R. Frank, *Omni,* May, 1979

14 If not controlled, work will flow to the competent man until he submerges.
　　　　— Charles Boyle,
　　　　Time, Feb. 26, 1979

15 Everyone must row with the oars he has.
　　　　— English proverb

16 'Tis skill, not strength, that governs a ship.
　　　　— Thomas Fuller, *Gnomologia,*
　　　　1732, no. 5116

17 The new enterprise equalizers are the intangible talents of the entrepreneur: enthusiasm, endurance, conclusiveness, leadership, product pride, marketing skills, nerve, and shrewdness.
　　　　— Deaver Brown,
　　　　The Entrepreneur's Guide,
　　　　1980, ch. 1

18 Those who apply themselves too closely to little things often become incapable of great things.
　　　　— François, Duc de la
　　　　Rochefoucauld, *Reflections;*
　　　　or, Sentences and Moral
　　　　Maxims, 1665, maxim 41

19 You have what a demagogue requires: a brutal voice, low birth, bad training. Why, you have all one wants for public life.
　　　　— Aristophanes, *The Knights,*
　　　　ca. 425 B.C., line 217

20 My meaning in saying he is a good man is to have you understand me that he is sufficient.
　　　　— William Shakespeare,
　　　　The Merchant of Venice, 1596,
　　　　act I, scene iii, line 15

21 The business ability of the man at the head of any business concern, big or little, is usually the factor which fixes the gulf between striking success and hopeless failure.
　　　　— Theodore Roosevelt,
　　　　quoted by Robert W. Kent,
　　　　Money Talks, 1985,
　　　　"Managers"

22 As the tempo of man's activity steadily increases, it is evident that men must become skilled practitioners of the science of selection.
　　　　— Philip Marvin,
　　　　Developing Decisions for Action,
　　　　1971, preface

23 You cannot define talent. All you can do is build the greenhouse and see if it grows.
　　　　— William P. Steven,
　　　　Time, Aug. 23, 1963

24 Everyone has talent. What is rare is the courage to follow the talent to the dark place where it leads.
　　　　— Erica Jong,
　　　　Los Angeles Times,
　　　　Feb. 3, 1978

25 An idea can turn into dust or magic, depending on the talent that rubs against it.
— William Bernbach,
New York Times,
Oct. 6, 1982

26 Every man loves what he is good at.
— Thomas Shadwell,
A True Widow, 1679,
act V, scene i

Achievement

27 *Achievement, n.* the death of endeavor and the birth of disgust.
— Ambrose Bierce,
The Devil's Dictionary, 1906

28 Knowledge may give weight, but accomplishments give lustre, and many more people see than weigh.
— Philip D.S. Chesterfield,
letter, May 8, 1750

29 Credentials are not the same as accomplishments.
— Robert Half, *Robert Half on Hiring,* 1985, ch. 2

30 There is no harm in wanting to accomplish; the harm is in having to accomplish.
— Hugh Prather, quoted by Robert W. Kent,
Money Talks, 1985,
"Microeconomics"

31 The trouble with most of us is that we stop trying in trying times.
— Denis Waitley and
Remi L. Witt, *The Joy of Working,* 1985, Day 7,
"Perseverance"

32 People who are really goal conscious don't spin their wheels. Their purpose is not to look and feel busy, but to achieve.
— Edwin C. Bliss, *Doing It Now,* 1986, Step 10:
"Manage Your Time"

33 Who reflects too much will accomplish little.
— Johann Christoph Friedrich von Schiller, *William Tell,*
1804, act III, scene i

34 The awareness of the ambiguity of one's highest achievements (as well as one's deepest failures) is a definite symptom of maturity.
— Paul Tillich, *Time,*
May 17, 1963

35 Some men go through life absolutely miserable because, despite the most enormous achievement, they just don't do one thing.
— Peter Thorneycroft,
London Sunday Telegraph,
Feb. 11, 1979

36 You don't have to do things. Maybe by avoiding doing things you accomplish a lot.
— Edmund G. Brown, Jr.,
New York Times,
April 26, 1976

37 Do just once what others say you can't do, and you will never pay attention to their limitations again.
— James R. Cook,
The Start-Up Entrepreneur,
1986, ch. 3

38 Nothing is ever accomplished by a reasonable man.
— J. Fred Bucy, quoted by Robert W. Kent,
Money Talks, 1985,
"Entrepreneurs"

39 If, in each matter, you look to all possible chances, never will you achieve anything. Far better it is to have a stout heart always, and suffer one's share of evil.
— Herodotus, *The History,*
ca. 450 B.C., book VII,
chapter 50

40 Keep thy heart with all diligence; for out of it are the issues of life.
— Bible, Proverbs 4:23

41 Seest thou a man diligent in his business? he shall stand before kings.
— Bible, Proverbs 22:29

42 People want to make a commitment to a purpose, a goal, a vision that is bigger than themselves — big enough to make them stretch and grow until they assume personal responsibility for achieving it.
— John Naisbitt and
Patricia Aburdene,
Re-inventing the Corporation,
1985, conclusion

43 You're in the front door, kid. What you do on this side of it is up to you.
— A.J. Carothers, *The Secret of My Success,* 1987

44 It's amazing what ordinary people can do if they set out without preconceived notions.
— Charles F. Kettering,
quoted by Peter Potter,
All About Success,
1988, "Habit"

45 If you tell people where to go, but not how to get there, you'll be amazed at the results.
— George S. Patton, quoted by
Roger von Oechs, *A Whack on the Side of the Head,*
1983, ch. 5

46 The great pleasure in life is doing what people say you cannot do.
— Walter Bagehot,
quoted by Peter Potter,
All About Success, 1988,
"Challenge"

47 If you do something once, people will call it an accident. If you do it twice, they call it a coincidence. But do it a third time and you've just proven a natural law.
— Grace Murray Hopper, quoted in *Mothers of Invention,* 1988, "From Eggbeaters to Eggheads"

48 If you can't measure output, then you measure input.
— Charles Schultze, *Washingtonian,* Nov., 1978

49 An organization where accountability is demanded will perform above average. This is the key to quality management.
— Vincent Vinci, *Sky* Magazine, Nov., 1986

50 The desire accomplished is sweet to the soul.
— Bible, Proverbs 13:19

51 There is no penalty for overachievement.
— George W. Miller, *Time,* July 17, 1978

52 No good deed will go unpunished.
— Walter Annenberg, *Poughkeepsie Journal,* March 26, 1978

Action

53 Shelving hard decisions is the least ethical course.
— Adrian Cadbury, *Harvard Business Review,* Sept./Oct., 1987

54 Action is the proper fruit of knowledge.
— Thomas Fuller, *Gnomologia,* 1732, no. 760

55 Every obnoxious act is a cry for help.
— Zig Ziglar, *Top Performance,* 1982, ch. 1

56 No one may contradict his own deed.
— The Universal Self-Instructor, 1883, "Legal Maxims"

57 Desire and force between them are responsible for all our action: desire causes our voluntary acts, forces our involuntary.
— Blaise Pascal, *Pensées,* 1670, no. 97

58 Efficiency is doing things right. Effectiveness is doing the right thing.
— Zig Ziglar, *Top Performance,* 1982, ch. 12

59 He who is permitted to do the greater may, with greater reason, do the less.
— The Universal Self-Instructor, 1883, "Legal Maxims"

60 What pity 'tis one that can speak so well
Should in his actions be so ill!
— Philip Massinger,
The Parliament of Love,
1624, act III, scene iii

61 One can relish the varied idiocy of human action during a panic to the full, for, while it is a time of great tragedy, nothing is being lost but money.
— John Kenneth Galbraith,
The Great Crash, 1929,
1955, ch. 1

62 In each action we must look beyond the action at our past, present, and future state, and at others whom it affects, and see the relations of all those things. And then we shall be very cautious.
— Blaise Pascal, *Pensées,*
1670, no. 505

63 Things have to be *made* to happen in the way you want them to happen. Without management, without the intervention of organized willpower, the desired result simply cannot be obtained.
— Robert Heller,
The Super Managers,
1984, epilogue

64 Why should we be cowed by the name of Action? 'Tis a trick of the senses, no more.

We know that the ancestor of every action is a thought.
— Ralph Waldo Emerson,
Essays: First Series,
1841, "Spiritual Laws"

65 A man of action forced into a state of thought is unhappy until he can get out of it.
— John Galsworthy,
Maid in Waiting,
1931, ch. 3

66 That action is best which procures the greatest happiness for the greatest numbers.
— Francis Hutcheson, *Inquiry Concerning Moral Good and Evil,* 1720, section 3

67 Man is only truly great when he acts from the passions.
— Benjamin Disraeli, *Coningsby,*
1844, book IV, ch. 13

68 People are always blaming their circumstances for what they are. I don't believe in circumstances. The people who get on in this world are the people who get up and look for the circumstances they want, and if they can't find them, make them.
— George Bernard Shaw,
Mrs. Warren's Profession,
1893, act II

69 The lure of the crisis is almost irresistible, because it demands your immediate attention. But in retrospect, it is the

high-priority items that count.
— Mitchell J. Posner, *Executive Essentials,* 1982, ch. 2

70 There are three arts which are concerned with all things: one which uses, another which makes, a third which imitates them.
— Plato, *The Republic,* ca. 370 B.C., book X, section 601

71 Knowledge must come through action; you can have no test which is not fanciful, save by trial.
— Sophocles, *Trachiniae,* ca. 430 B.C., line 592

72 For the things we have to learn before we can do them, we learn by doing them.
Aristotle, *Nicomachean Ethics,* ca. 330 B.C., book II, ch. 1

73 Everywhere in life the true question is, not what we have gained, but what we do.
— Thomas Carlyle, quoted by Peter Potter, *All About Success,* 1988, "Achievement"

Advice

74 *Advice, n.* the smallest current coin.
— Ambrose Bierce, *The Devil's Dictionary,* 1906

75 Good counselors lack no clients.
— William Shakespeare, *Measure for Measure,* 1605, act I, scene ii, line 115

76 There is nothing which we receive with so much reluctance as advice.
— Joseph Addison, *The Spectator,* 1711-1712, no. 512

77 If you want people to notice your faults, start giving advice.
— Kelly Stephens, *Reader's Digest,* Feb., 1967

78 When a man asks your advice, he usually tells you just how he expects you to decide.
— Edgar Watson Howe, *Country Town Sayings,* 1911

79 Advice is not disliked because it is advice, but because so few people know how to give it.
— Leigh Hunt, *The Indicator,* 1821, no. 51

80 We are so happy to advise others that occasionally, we even do it in their interest.
— Jules Renard, *Journal,* 1887-1910

81 Don't ask a barber if you need a haircut.
— Daniel Greenberg, *Wall Street Journal,* Sept. 18, 1977

82 When a dog is drowning, everyone offers him a drink.
— George Herbert,
Jacula Prudentum,
1651, no. 77

83 A blind man will not thank you for a looking-glass.
— Thomas Fuller,
Gnomologia, 1732, no. 18

84 Advice after injury is like medicine after death.
— Danish proverb

Agreement

85 Consensus is the security blanket of the insecure.
— Pierre A. Rinfret,
Challenge,
May/June, 1976

86 Can two walk together, except they be agreed?
— Bible, Amos 3:3

87 We rarely find that people have good sense unless they agree with us.
— François, Duc de la Rochefoucauld, *Reflections; or, Sentences and Moral Maxims,* 1665, maxim 347

88 Familiarity breeds acceptance.
— Eliot F. Noyes, *Time,*
Aug. 1, 1977

89 Sympathy of manners maketh conjunction of minds.
— Thomas Fuller,
Gnomologia, 1732, no. 4300

90 How agree the kettle and the earthen pot together?
— Bible: Apocrypha,
Ecclesiasticus 13:2

91 Many promising reconciliations have broken down because, while both parties came prepared to forgive, neither party came prepared to be forgiven.
— Charles Williams,
quoted by Robert W. Kent,
Money Talks, 1985,
"Communications"

92 The difficulty about a gentlemen's agreement is that it depends on the continued existence of the gentlemen.
— Reginald Withers Payne,
New York Times,
Feb. 9, 1964

93 Ah, don't say that you agree with me. When people agree with me, I always feel that I must be wrong.
— Oscar Wilde,
Lady Windermere's Fan,
1892, act II

Appearances

94 Advancement often depends not on rightness of action, but on acceptable behavior and image, e.g. self-control, appearance and dress,

perception as a team player, style and patron of power. The result of all this is ethical erosion.
— Robert W. Goddard, *Personnel Journal,* March, 1988

95 A fair exterior is a silent recommendation.
— Publilius Syrus, *Maxims,* 1st Century B.C., no. 267

96 The greatest strength of some job candidates is their ability to impress the people who interview them.
— Robert Half, *Robert Half on Hiring,* 1985, ch. 8

97 Every true man's apparel fits your thief.
— William Shakespeare, *Measure for Measure,* 1605, act IV, scene ii, line 46

98 A man in business must put up many fronts if he loves his own quiet.
— William Penn, quoted by Robert W. Kent, *Money Talks,* 1985, "Managers"

99 A resume is a balance sheet without any liabilities.
— Robert Half, *Robert Half on Hiring,* 1985, ch. 4

100 Always behave like a duck — keep calm and unruffled on the surface but paddle like the devil underneath.
— Jacob Braude, quoted by Peter Potter, *All About Success,* 1988, "Appearances"

Attitude

101 If you think you can, you can. And if you think you can't, you're right.
— Mary Kay Ash, *New York Times,* Oct. 20, 1985

102 Your attitude is a choice you make.
— Denis Waitley and Remi L. Witt, *The Joy of Working,* 1985, "Day 3, Attitude"

103 The love of glory, the fear of disgrace, the incentive to succeed, the desire to live in comfort, and the instinct to humiliate others are often the cause of that courage so renowned among men.
— François, Duc de la Rochefoucauld, *Reflections; or, Sentences and Moral Maxims,* 1665, maxim 213

104 A great society is a society in which its men of business think greatly of their functions.
— Alfred North Whitehead, quoted by Robert W. Kent, *Money Talks,* 1985, "Business Is and Business As"

105 "The firm"—a proud Victorian word. It evokes the lost sense of Victorian regard for the pride of people in their daily trade.
—V.S. Pritchett,
New Yorker Magazine,
June 24, 1985

106 A bad attitude is the worst thing that can happen to a group of people. It's infectious.
—Roger Allen Raby,
Wall Street Journal,
April 12, 1984

107 I never knew so young a body with so old a head.
—William Shakespeare,
The Merchant of Venice, 1596,
act IV, scene i, line 163

108 Because of indifference, one dies before one actually dies.
—Elie Wiesel,
U.S. News and World Report,
Oct. 27, 1986

109 A man is not finished when he is defeated. He is finished when he quits.
—Richard M. Nixon,
Dallas Times-Herald,
Dec. 10, 1978

110 Men who are "orthodox" when they are young are in danger of being middle-aged all their lives.
—Walter Lippman,
Harvard Monthly, 1910

111 Human beings are perhaps never more frightening than when they are convinced beyond doubt that they are right.
—Laurens Van der Post,
The Lost World of the Kalahari, 1958, ch. 3

112 Your business is never really good or bad out there. Your business is either good or bad between your own two ears.
—Zig Ziglar, *Secrets of Closing the Sale,* 1984, ch. 9

113 One of the best-kept secrets in America is that people are aching to make a commitment—if they only had the freedom and environment in which to do so.
—John Naisbitt and Patricia Aburdene, *Re-inventing the Corporation,* 1985, conclusion

114 Don't hire anybody over thirty-five years old with ten or more years in a big union. It's not worth the effort to turn them around so they're working for you instead of against you.
—Robert Townsend, *Further Up the Organization,* 1984, "Big Labor Unions: Sounds of the Dying Dinosaur"

115 The key element in good business management is

emotional attitude. The rest is mechanics.
— Harold Geneen with
Alvin Moscow, *Managing,*
1984, ch. 13

116 The other person's attitude depends on which direction the money moves between you.
— Leo Nova, *Omni,*
May, 1979

117 The point of view that we can be without a point of view is a point of view.
— Gary Zukav, *The Dancing Wu Li Masters: An Overview of the New Physics,* 1980

Belief

118 Never take anything for granted.
— Benjamin Disraeli,
speech
Oct. 5, 1864

119 He does not believe that does not live according to his belief.
— Thomas Fuller,
Gnomologia,
1732, no. 1838

120 To believe is very dull. To doubt is intensely engrossing.
— Oscar Wilde,
Oscariana, 1911

121 Objection of atheists: "But we have no light."
— Blaise Pascal,
Pensées,
1670, no. 228

122 No one has ever died an atheist.
— Plato, *Laws,* ca. 350 B.C.,
book X, section 888

123 If a man could kill all his illusions he'd become a god.
— Colin Wilson,
Ritual in the Dark, 1960

124 It is necessary to the happiness of man that he be mentally faithful to himself. Infidelity does not consist in disbelieving, it consists in professing to believe what one does not believe.
— Thomas Paine,
The Age of Reason,
1794, part I

125 Desire is indeed powerful; it engenders belief.
— Marcel Proust,
Remembrance of Things Past,
1913–1926, volume VI,
"The Sweet Cheat Gone"

126 A man who is always ready to believe what is told him will never do well.
— Gaius Petronius,
Satyricon,
ca. A.D. 65, section 43

127 Believing is seeing. It's much more effective than the old notion that seeing is believing.
— Terrence E. Deal and Allen A. Kennedy, *Corporate Cultures,* 1982, ch. 5

128 The most costly of all follies is to believe passionately in the palpably not true. It is the chief occupation of mankind.
— H.L. Mencken, *A Mencken Chrestomathy,* 1949

129 Just as no one can be forced into belief, so no one can be forced into unbelief.
— Sigmund Freud, *The Ego and the Id,* 1923, page 55

130 The majority of people believe in incredible things which are absolutely false. The majority of people daily act in a manner prejudicial to their general well-being.
— Ashley Montagu, *In Fact,* newsletter, 1940

131 He who begins life by stifling his convictions is in a fair way to ending it without any convictions to stifle.
— John Morley, *On Compromise,* 1874, ch. 3

132 A precedent embalms a principle.
— Benjamin Disraeli, speech, House of Commons, Feb. 22, 1848

133 Underlying the whole scheme of civilization is the confidence men have in each other, confidence in their integrity, confidence in their honesty, confidence in their future.
— W. Bourke Cockran, speech, Aug. 18, 1896

134 One person with a belief is a social power equal to ninety-nine who have only interests.
— John Stuart Mill, *Representative Government,* 1861, ch. 8

Bores and Boredom

135 The hardest knife ill-used doth lose its edge.
— William Shakespeare, sonnet 95, 1609

136 As you get better at a thing, it gets less interesting.
— Jim Slater, *The Observer,* Sept. 24, 1978

137 The thoughtless are rarely wordless.
— Howard W. Newton, quoted by Peter Potter, *All About Success,* 1988, "Thought"

138 It is the dull man who is always sure, and the sure man who is always dull.
— H.L. Mencken,
Prejudices, Second Series,
1920, ch. 1

139 Highly educated bores are by far the worst; they know so much, in such fiendish detail, to be boring about.
— Louis Kronenberger,
Forbes,
May 1, 1964

140 A vain man may become proud and imagine himself pleasing to all when he is in reality a universal nuisance.
— Baruch Spinoza,
Ethics, 1677,
part III, proposition 30

141 The worst sin is dullness.
— David H.C. Read,
Time, Dec. 31, 1979

142 Boredom is a vital problem for the moralist, since at least half the sins of mankind are caused by the fear of it.
— Bertrand Russell,
The Conquest of Happiness,
1930, ch. 4

143 The man who lets himself be bored is even more contemptible than the bore.
— Samuel Butler,
The Fair Haven, 1873,
"The Memoir," ch. 3

144 The state of man: inconstancy, boredom, anxiety.
— Blaise Pascal,
Pensées,
1670, no. 127

145 Every hero becomes a bore at last.
— Ralph Waldo Emerson,
Time, June 9, 1978

Budgets

146 You don't need an M.B.A. from Harvard to figure out how to lose money.
— Royal Little,
Best of Business Quarterly, 1987

147 Budgeting is a black art practiced by bureaucratic magicians.
— David Muchow,
Chicago Sun-Times,
Nov. 19, 1976

148 If you don't appreciate the amount of luxuries your budget can afford, you are getting paid far too much.
— David A. Ogden,
Omni, May, 1979

149 A budget is a statement of priorities, and there's no more political document.
— Edward K. Hamilton,
New York Times, Feb. 9, 1971

150 Budgets are good for much more than estimating how much money you're going to

need to keep the ball rolling in your department. If they are prepared well and used properly, they can also be effective tools for discovering and cutting unnecessary expenses.
— *Supervisor's Bulletin,*
Jan. 30, 1987,
number 750

151 So soon as we begin to count the cost, the cost begins.
— Henry David Thoreau,
Winter, Jan. 18, 1841

152 Budgets, as a whole, are not taken seriously and no other usable system of control has emerged. That is why a great many organizations get into financial trouble without realizing it early enough.
— Philip B. Crosby,
Running Things,
1986, ch. 10

153 Like all other techniques of business, the budget should be a door open to more satisfying and profitable work — not an instrument of torture.
— James L. Pierce,
Harvard Business Review, 1954

154 When a manager makes up a budget for the coming year, he is putting down on paper a series of expectations, expressed in numbers.
— Harold Geneen,
Fortune, Oct. 1, 1984

155 Profits don't just happen — they must be planned. A good profit planning and control system (budget) lies at the heart of profitable organizations.
— Joel E. Ross and
Michael J. Kami,
*Corporate Management
in Crisis: Why the
Mighty Fall,* 1973, ch. 12

156 Top management tends to ask the wrong questions about a proposed increase in the advertising budget. They tend to ask: "What's the return on the investment?" Instead they should ask, "How much do we have to spend to ensure victory?"
— Al Ries and Jack Trout,
Marketing Warfare, 1986, ch. 12

157 Since a division must believe in the budget as its own plan for operations, management cannot juggle figures just because it likes to. Any changes must be sold to the division or the whole process is a sham.
— Robert Townsend,
Further Up the Organization,
1984, "Budgets"

158 Balancing the budget is a little like protecting your virtue — you just have to learn to say no.
— Ronald Reagan, quoted by
Gerald Gardner, *All the
Presidents' Wits,* 1986, ch. 5

Bureaucracy

159 *Egypt:* where the Israelites would still be if Moses had been a bureaucrat.
— Laurence J. Peter,
The Peter Pyramid,
1986, ch. 1

160 We need to revise the old saying to read, Hell hath no fury like a bureaucrat scorned.
— Milton Friedman,
Newsweek,
Dec. 29, 1975

161 Bureaucrats are the only people in the world who can say absolutely nothing and mean it.
— Hugh Sidey, *Time,*
Nov. 29, 1976

162 Making something perfectly clear only confuses everybody.
— George Rockwell,
Down East,
Jan., 1976

163 Most bureaucratic regulations look like Chinese to me — and I can read Chinese.
— W. Michael Blumenthal,
Washingtonian,
Aug., 1977

164 Any argument worth making within the bureaucracy must be capable of being expressed in a simple declarative sentence that is obviously true once stated.
— John McNaughton,
Wall Street Journal, March 3, 1974

165 The difference between management and administration (which is what the bureaucrats used to do exclusively) is the difference between choice and rigidity.
— Robert Heller,
The Super Managers,
1984, epilogue

166 The measurement of the gestation period of an original thought in a bureaucracy is still pending.
— Hugh Sidey, *Time,*
Nov. 29, 1976

167 The perfect bureaucrat everywhere is the man who manages to make no decisions and escape all responsibility.
— Brooks Atkinson,
Once Around the Sun, 1951

168 It's a poor bureaucrat who can't stall a good idea until even its sponsor is relieved to see it dead and officially buried.
— Robert Townsend, *Further Up the Organization,* 1984, "Ejaculation, Premature"

169 When a bureaucrat makes a mistake and continues to make it, it usually becomes the new policy.
— Hugh Sidey, *Time,*
Nov. 29, 1976

170 Guidelines for Bureaucrat: (1) When in charge ponder. (2) When in trouble delegate. (3) When in doubt mumble.
—James H. Boren,
quoted by Peter Potter,
All About Success, 1988,
"The Right Stuff"

171 Bureaucracy is nothing more than a hardening of an organization's arteries.
—William P. Anthony,
Managing Incompetence,
1981, ch. 9

172 Bureaucracy defends the status quo long past the time when the quo has lost its status.
—Laurence J. Peter,
San Francisco Chronicle,
Jan. 29, 1978

173 In a bureaucratic system, increase in expenditure will be matched by fall in production.
—Max Gammon,
Newsweek, Nov. 7, 1977

174 All autonomous agencies and authorities, sooner or later, turn into self-perpetuating strongholds of conventional thought and practice.
—Ada Louise Huxtable,
New York Times,
Aug. 22, 1971

175 The only hope for the human race is for the rate of population increase to continue to exceed that of bureaucratic growth.
—Arthur H. Robinson,
Albany Times-Union,
July 6, 1975

176 Bureaucracy, the rule of no one, has become the modern form of despotism.
—Mary McCarthy,
New Yorker Magazine,
Oct. 18, 1958

177 Issues are the last refuges of scoundrels.
—Edmund G. Brown, Jr.,
Washingtonian, Nov., 1979

178 The enemy of the market is not ideology but the engineer.
—John Kenneth Galbraith,
The New Industrial State,
1967, ch. 3

179 It is because we put up with bad things that hotel-keepers continue to give them to us.
—Anthony Trollope,
Orley Farm, 1862, ch. 18

180 I am ashamed to think how easily we capitulate to badges and names, to large societies and dead institutions.
—Ralph Waldo Emerson,
Essays: First Series,
1841, "Self-Reliance"

181 For every action there is an equal and opposite government program.
— Michael Main,
Omni, May, 1979

182 There is good news from Washington today. Congress is deadlocked and can't act.
— Will Rogers,
Newsweek, June 9, 1975

183 Public money is like holy water; everyone helps himself.
— Italian proverb

184 This island is almost made of coal and surrounded by fish. Only an organizing genius could produce a shortage of coal and fish in Great Britain at the same time.
— Aneurin Bevan,
speech, May 18, 1945

185 Be careful of corporate deadwood. Ask yourself: Are all these fat cats in staff really necessary?
— Joel E. Ross and
Michael J. Kami,
*Corporate Management
in Crisis: Why the
Mighty Fall,* 1973, ch. 19

186 As work and space expand and collide they breed their own reaction.
— Haynes Johnson,
Washington Post,
Aug. 14, 1977

187 Remember that in the well-articulated bureaucracy, work tends to be watered down to fit the size of the staff.
— Woodrow H. Sears, Jr.,
Back in Working Order,
1984, ch. 4

188 There is something about a bureaucracy that does not like a poem.
— Gore Vidal,
Sex, Death and Money,
1968, preface

189 The volume of paper expands to fill the available briefcases.
— Edmund G. Brown, Jr.,
Wall Street Journal,
Feb. 26, 1976

190 Skewered through and through with office pens, and bound hand and foot with red tape.
— Charles Dickens,
David Copperfield,
1850, ch. 43

191 We can lick gravity, but sometimes the paperwork is overwhelming.
— Wernher von Braun,
Chicago Sun-Times,
July 10, 1958

Buying

192 The seeds of every company's demise are contained in its business plan.
— Fred Adler,
Inc. Magazine, Feb., 1987

193 Never buy anything you can't lift.
—John Bear,
Computer Wimp,
1983, ch. 2

194 People don't buy for logical reasons. They buy for emotional reasons.
—Zig Ziglar,
Secrets of Closing the Sale,
1984, ch. 21

195 We are continually buying something that we never get, from a man that never had it.
—Will Rogers, quoted by Richard M. Ketchum,
Will Rogers, His Life and Times,
1973, page 267

196 Possession diminishes perception of value, immediately.
—John Updike,
New Yorker,
Nov. 3, 1975

197 People buy what they want when they want it more than they want the money it costs.
—Zig Ziglar,
Secrets of Closing the Sale,
1984, ch. 2

198 The buyer needs a hundred eyes, the seller not one.
—George Herbert,
Jacula Prudentum,
1651, no. 390

199 Don't buy a $10,000 solid gold sledgehammer to drive in a two-cent thumb tack.
—John Bear,
Computer Wimp,
1983, ch. 3

Change

200 It is only the wisest and most stupid who cannot change.
—Confucius, *Analects,*
ca. 500 B.C.,
book XVII, ch. 3

201 Anything new, anything worth doing, can't be recognized. People just don't have that much vision.
—Pablo Picasso,
Saturday Review,
May 28, 1966

202 Every reform, however necessary, will by weak minds be carried to an excess, that itself will need reforming.
—Samuel Taylor Coleridge,
Biographia Literaria,
1817, ch. 1

203 Beware of all enterprises that require new clothes.
—Henry David Thoreau,
Walden, 1854, 1, "Economy"

204 The human mind likes a strange idea as little as the body

likes a strange protein and resists it with a similar energy.
— W.I. Beveridge, quoted by Roger von Oech, *A Kick in the Seat of the Pants,* 1986, "The Judge"

205 Even in slight things the experience of the new is rarely without some stirring of foreboding.
— Eric Hoffer, *The Ordeal of Change,* 1963, ch. 1

206 Avoid organizational rigor mortis. Change is inevitable and the organization — and its people — must accommodate change.
— Joel E. Ross and Michael J. Kami, *Corporate Management in Crisis: Why the Mighty Fall,* 1973, ch. 18

207 If in the last few years you hadn't discarded a major opinion or acquired a new one, check your pulse. You may be dead.
— Gelett Burgess, *Forbes,* Aug. 1, 1977

208 Change is inevitable in a progressive society. Change is constant.
— Benjamin Disraeli, speech, Oct. 20, 1867

209 In their search for quality, people seem to be looking for permanency in a time of change.
— John Naisbitt and Patricia Aburdene, *Re-inventing the Corporation,* 1985, ch. 2

210 Men come and go as leaves year by year upon the trees. Those of autumn the wind sheds upon the ground, but when spring returns the forest buds forth with fresh ones.
— Homer, *The Iliad,* ca. 550 B.C., book VI, line 146

211 Developing a compiler was a logical move; but in matters like this, you don't run against logic — you run against people who can't change their minds.
— Grace Murray Hopper, quoted in *Mothers of Invention,* 1988, "From Eggbeaters to Eggheads"

212 Can you teach the crab to walk straight? You cannot.
— Aristophanes, *The Peace,* ca. 425 B.C., line 1083

213 There are no right or wrong characteristics, no good or bad characteristics. We are where we are and what we are because of what has gone into our minds. We change where we are and what we are by changing what goes into our minds.

—Zig Ziglar,
Top Performance,
1982, ch. 10

214 A manager, no matter how brilliant, cannot alone achieve acceptance of and support for a change from those affected or otherwise involved. To do so, he must depend on others.

—Arnold S. Judson,
A Manager's Guide to Making Changes, 1967, preface

215 Change occurs when there is a confluence of both changing values and economic necessity, not before.

—John Naisbitt,
Megatrends, 1984, ch. 7

216 Excessive dependence on past policies, however successful, is dangerous in time of rapid change.

—Joel E. Ross and
Michael J. Kami,
*Corporate Management
in Crisis: Why the
Mighty Fall,* 1973, ch. 9

217 Any worthwhile action creates change. Feedback from this change initiates recycling of the decision-making process.

Decision making must function as a free form process. It must be responsive to change.

—Philip Marvin,
*Developing Decisions for
Action,* 1971, ch. 13

218 And it is great
To do that thing that ends all other deeds,
Which shackles accidents, and bolts up change.

—William Shakespeare,
Antony and Cleopatra, 1607,
act V, scene ii, line 4

219 When a company or an individual compromises one time, whether it's on price or on principle, the next compromise is right around the corner and you can bet your last nickel on it.

—Zig Ziglar,
Secrets of Closing the Sale,
1984, ch. 18

220 Like all weak men, he laid an exaggerated stress on not changing one's mind.

—William Somerset Maugham,
Of Human Bondage,
1915, ch. 39

221 If you want to make enemies, try to change something.

—Woodrow Wilson,
speech, July 10, 1916

Character

222 Character is that which can do without success.
— Ralph Waldo Emerson,
Essays: Second Series,
1844, "Character"

223 A bad reference is as hard to find as a good employee.
— Robert Half,
Robert Half on Hiring,
1985, ch. 9

224 Men's natures are alike; it is their habits that carry them apart.
— Confucius, *Analects,*
ca. 500 B.C.,
book XVII, ch. 2

225 You've got to learn to survive a defeat. That's when you develop character.
— Richard M. Nixon,
Dallas Times-Herald,
Dec. 10, 1978

226 The just upright man is laughed to scorn.
— Bible, Job 12:4

227 Character is tested by true sentiments more than by conduct. A man is seldom better than his word.
— John E.E. Dalberg,
letter, April 5, 1887

228 If a man's character is to be abused, say what you will,

there's nobody like a relation to do the business.
— William Makepeace
Thackeray, *Vanity Fair,*
1847, ch. 19

229 Many would be cowards if they had courage enough.
— Thomas Fuller,
Gnomologia,
1732, no. 3366

230 The analysis of character is the highest human entertainment.
— Isaac Bashevis Singer,
New York Times,
Nov. 26, 1978

231 Many people have character who have nothing else.
— Don Herold,
Chicago Sun-Times,
July 14, 1979

232 There are only two kinds of men: those righteous who believe themselves sinners; the other sinners who believe themselves righteous.
— Blaise Pascal, *Pensées,*
1670, no. 562

233 There may be said to be two classes of people in the world: those who constantly divide the people of the world into two classes and those who do not.
— Robert Benchley,
Washingtonian,
Nov., 1978

Communication

234 Incomprehensible jargon is the hallmark of a profession.
— Kingman Brewster, Jr.,
speech, Dec. 13, 1977

235 Never forget what a man says to you when he is angry.
— Henry Ward Beecher,
quoted by Peter Potter, *All About Success*, 1988, "Anger"

236 Teleconferencing is so rational, it will never succeed.
— John Naisbitt,
Megatrends,
1984, ch. 2

237 There is no such thing as a worthless conversation, providing you know what to listen for. And questions are the breath of life for a conversation.
— James Nathan Miller,
Reader's Digest,
Sept., 1965

238 The most bloodthirsty language in the newspapers today is not found in the international pages. It's found in the business pages.
— Al Ries and Jack Trout,
Marketing Warfare,
1986, ch. 4

239 Ours is the age of substitutes; instead of language, we have jargon; instead of principles, slogans; instead of genuine ideas, Bright ideas.
— Eric Bentley,
The Dramatic Event, 1954

240 When two men communicate with each other by word of mouth, there is a twofold hazard in that communication.
— Sam Ervin,
New York Times,
July 13, 1973

241 Half the world is composed of people who have something to say and can't, and the other half who have nothing to say and keep on saying it.
— Robert Frost,
Kansas City Star,
July 14, 1977

242 Nowadays to be intelligible is to be found out.
— Oscar Wilde,
Lady Windermere's Fan,
1892, act III

243 We have found that many "modern" managers only deal with the tip of the iceberg as far as communications are concerned.
— Terrence E. Deal and
Allen A. Kennedy,
Corporate Cultures, 1982, ch. 5

244 Can't you see that for mighty thoughts and heroic

aims, the words themselves must be appropriate?
— Aristophanes,
The Frogs,
ca. 405 B.C., line 1057

245 It is a foolish thing to make a long prologue, and to be short in the story itself.
— Bible: Apocrypha,
II Maccabees 2:32

246 Not that the story need be long, but it will take a while to make it short.
— Henry David Thoreau,
letter, Nov. 16, 1857

247 An honest tale speeds best being plainly told.
— William Shakespeare,
Richard III, 1593,
act IV, scene iv, line 359

248 Let thy speech be short, comprehending much in few words.
— Bible: Apocrypha,
Ecclesiasticus 32:8

249 It is when I struggle to be brief that I become obscure.
— Horace, *Epistles III,*
ca. 10 B.C., line 25

250 If I take refuge in ambiguity, I assure you that it's quite conscious.
— Kingman Brewster,
New York Herald,
Oct. 14, 1963

251 What is the short meaning of the long speech?
— Johann Christoph
Friedrich von Schiller,
Die Piccolomini, 1799,
act I, scene ii

252 [a] "Write task descriptions as simply and briefly as possible."
— Anonymous (from a procedure for writing procedures — first draft)

[b] "When developing narrative descriptions of functional activities intended as communicative vehicles for instructive documentation, it is incumbent upon the cognizant supervisory personnel to ensure that non-technical methodologies of expression are employed."
— Anonymous (as redrafted by a management consultant)

253 Good communication is characterized by providing employees with information which they want and getting information to them quickly and through the channels they prefer.
— Louis I. Gelfand,
Harvard Business Review, 1970

254 All erroneous ideas would perish of their own accord if expressed clearly.
— Luc de Clapiers, *Reflections and Maxims,* ca. 1747

255 One of the best ways to persuade others is with your ears — by listening to them.
— Dean Rusk,
Reader's Digest, July, 1961

256 No one has a finer command of language than the person who keeps his mouth shut.
— Sam Rayburn,
Lawrence Daily Journal-World,
Aug. 29, 1978

257 Don't hide your strategy under a bushel. Communicate it throughout your company. Make it all pervasive and let it set a tone and a character to your organization. It's better today to disclose too much than too little.
— Joel E. Ross and
Michael J. Kami,
*Corporate Management
in Crisis: Why the
Mighty Fall,* 1973, ch. 10

258 You have not converted a man, because you have silenced him.
— John Morley,
On Compromise,
1874, ch. 3

259 American society is composed of an intricate web of institutional affiliations so inclusive that, it has been alleged, anyone in the United States can be found by making seven phone calls.
— Woodrow H. Sears, Jr.,
Back in Working Order, 1984,
introduction

260 The responsiveness of a firm to the consumer is directly proportionate to the distance on the organization chart from the consumer to the chairman of the board.
— Virginia H. Knauer,
quoted by Robert W. Kent,
Money Talks, 1985,
"Communications"

261 They have mouths, but they speak not: eyes have they, but they see not.
They have ears, but they hear not.
— Bible, Psalm 115:5-6

262 We rarely confide in those who are better than we are.
— Albert Camus,
The Fall, 1956

263 No man delights in the bearer of bad news.
— Sophocles, *Antigone,*
ca. 440 B.C., line 277

Competition

264 New York is just like Kansas — intensified.
— A.J. Carothers, *The Secret
of My Success,* 1987

265 Nobody talks more of free enterprise and competition and of the best man winning than the man who inherited his father's store or farm.
—C. Wright Mills, quoted by Robert W. Kent, *Money Talks,* 1985, "Business Is and Business As"

266 I don't meet the competition. I crush it.
—Charles Revson, *Time,* June 16, 1958

267 The biggest mistake marketing people make is failing to appreciate the strength of a defensive position. The glamour of offensive war and the thrill of victory makes the average marketing manager eager to pick up a lance and go charging off at the nearest entrenched competitor.
—Al Ries and Jack Trout, *Marketing Warfare,* 1986, ch. 3

268 Business is a combination of war and sport.
—André Maurois, quoted by Robert W. Kent, *Money Talks,* 1985, "Business Is and Business As"

269 If you want to go out and do battle with your competitors, it's helpful to know where to go.
—Al Ries and Jack Trout, *Marketing Warfare,* 1986, ch. 5

270 We go to gain a little patch of ground
That hath in it no profit but the name.
—William Shakespeare, *Hamlet,* 1601, act IV, scene iv, line 18

271 Competition continually struggles trying to catch up. A moving target is harder to hit than a stationary one.
—Al Ries and Jack Trout, *Marketing Warfare,* 1986, ch. 7

272 People of the same trade seldom meet together, even for merriment and diversion, but the conversation ends in a conspiracy against the public, or in some contrivance to raise prices.
—Adam Smith, *Wealth of Nations,* 1776, Volume I, Book I, ch. 10, part 2

273 Anybody can win—unless there happens to be a second entry.
—George Ade, *Omni,* May, 1979

Computers

274 Don't expect the typewriter to ever completely disappear.
—Hal Fair, *New York Times,* Nov. 23, 1984

275 Not even computers will replace committees, because committees buy computers.
— Edward Shepherd Mead,
Wall Street Journal,
June 18, 1964

276 Skeptics used to greet pioneering motorists with the cry "get a horse." People who dismiss the impact of the personal computer, including many of the folks who use the machine, tend to employ the phrase, "It's just a tool."
— Peter Nulty,
Fortune Magazine,
Sept. 3, 1984

277 Computers are useless. They can only give you answers.
— Pablo Picasso, quoted by Robert Byrne, *The Other 637 Best Things Anybody Ever Said,* 1984, no. 623

278 Computerization requires a new type of manager. He has to be able to think about how he does something, rather than just do it.
— Marshall Evans,
Business Week,
June 25, 1966

279 The real problem is not whether machines think but whether men do.
— B.F. Skinner,
Contingencies of Reinforcement,
1969, ch. 9

280 A computer will do what you tell it to do, but that may be much different from what you had in mind.
— Joseph Weizenbaum,
Time, Feb. 20, 1978

281 Most of the computer technicians that you're likely to meet or hire are complicators, not simplifiers. They're trying to make it look tough, not easy. They're building a mystique, a priesthood, their own mumbo-jumbo ritual to keep you from knowing what they — and you — are doing.
— Robert Townsend, *Further Up the Organization,* 1984, "Computers and Their Priests"

282 Men are going to have to learn to be managers in a world where the organization will come close to consisting of all chiefs and one Indian. The Indian, of course, is the computer.
— Thomas L. Whisler,
Christian Science Monitor,
April 21, 1964

283 We are becoming the servants in thought, as in action, of the machine we have created to serve us.
— John Kenneth Galbraith,
The New Industrial State,
1967, ch. 1

284 Technology ... the knack of so arranging the world

that we don't have to experience it.

> —Max Frisch, quoted by
> Robert W. Kent,
> *Money Talks*, 1985,
> "Production and Operations"

285 The main impact of the computer has been the provision of unlimited jobs for clerks.

> —Peter F. Drucker,
> *New York Times*,
> May 16, 1976

286 Being in the microcomputer business is like going 55 miles an hour 3 feet from a cliff.

> —George Morrow,
> *Fortune*, April 14, 1986

287 Setting fire to one disk is a satisfying way of overcoming temporary computer hostility.

> —John Bear,
> *Computer Wimp*, 1983, ch. 5

Conflict

288 You may fight to the death for something in which you truly believe, but keep such commitments to a bare minimum.

> —Albert A. Grant,
> speech, May 30, 1988

289 Persuade me you may, but I won't be persuaded.

> —Aristophanes,
> *The Plutus*,
> ca. 390 B.C., line 600

290 No man thinks there is much ado about nothing when the ado is about himself.

> —Anthony Trollope,
> *The Bertrams*, 1859, ch. 27

291 He that hath the worst cause makes the most noise.

> —Thomas Fuller,
> *Gnomologia*, 1732, no. 2153

292 The quarrel is a very petty quarrel as it stands; we should only spoil it by trying to explain it.

> —Richard Brinsley Sheridan,
> *The Rivals*, 1775,
> act IV, scene iii

293 The test of a man or woman's breeding is how they behave in a quarrel.

> —George Bernard Shaw,
> *The Philanderer*,
> 1893, act IV

294 Arguments are to be avoided; they are always vulgar and often convincing.

> —Oscar Wilde,
> *The Importance of
> Being Earnest*, 1895, act II

295 There is no such thing as a convincing argument, although every man thinks he has one.

> —Edgar Watson Howe,
> *Country Town Sayings*, 1911

296 In a serious struggle there is no worse cruelty than to

be magnanimous at an inopportune time.
— Leon Trotsky, *The History of the Russian Revolution,* 1933, volume IV, ch. 7

297 Beware
Of entrance to a quarrel, but, being in,
Bear 't that th' opposed may beware of thee.
Give every man thy ear, but few thy voice;
Take each man's censure, but reserve thy judgment.
— William Shakespeare, *Hamlet,* 1601, act I, scene iii, line 65

298 The best way I know of to win an argument is to start by being in the right.
— Quinton M. Hogg, *New York Times,* Oct. 16, 1960

299 Adversity causes some men to break; others to break records.
— William A. Ward, quoted by Peter Potter, *All About Success,* 1988, "Adversity"

300 Difference of opinion leads to inquiry, and inquiry to truth.
— Thomas Jefferson, letter, March 13, 1815

301 To survive the day is triumph enough for the walk-

ing wounded among the great many of us.
— Studs Terkel, *Working,* 1972, introduction

302 My experience has been . . . that in the end, when you fight for a desperate cause and have good reasons to fight, you usually win.
— Edward Teller, *Wall Street Journal,* Aug. 8, 1986

303 If two men on the same job agree all the time, then one is useless. If they disagree all the time, then both are useless.
— Darryl F. Zanuck, *The Observer,* Oct. 23, 1949

304 Whoever deprives another of the right to state unpopular views necessarily deprives others of the right to listen to those views.
— C. Vann Woodward, *New York Times,* Jan. 28, 1975

305 Beware the financial man who does not have confrontations; a good financial man can be expected to have at least one confrontation every day.
— Henry O. Golightly, *Managing with Style,* 1977, ch. 2

306 The lion and the calf shall lie down together, but the calf won't get much sleep.
— Woody Allen,
Time, Feb. 26, 1979

307 There can be no covenants between men and lions; wolves and lambs can never be of one mind.
— Homer, *The Iliad,*
ca. 550 B.C.,
book XXII, line 262

308 Come not between the dragon and his wrath.
— William Shakespeare,
King Lear, 1606,
act I, scene i, line 124

309 The satisfied, the happy, do not live; they fall asleep from habit, near neighbor to annihilation.
— Miguel de Unamuno,
The Tragic Sense of Life,
1913, ch. 9

310 Many can bear adversity, but few contempt.
— Thomas Fuller,
Gnomologia,
1732, no. 3340

311 Silence . . . the unbearable repartee.
— Alexander Theros,
Reader's Digest,
May, 1983

312 Silence is the most perfect example of scorn.
— George Bernard Shaw,
Back to Methuselah,
1921, part V

313 Our doubts are traitors,
And make us lose the good we oft might win,
By fearing to attempt.
— William Shakespeare,
Measure for Measure, 1605,
act I, scene iv, line 78

314 The only things that evolve by themselves in an organization are disorder, friction and malperformance.
— Peter F. Drucker,
Wharton Magazine, Fall, 1976

315 No man can smile in the face of adversity and mean it.
— Edgar Watson Howe,
Country Town Sayings, 1911

Conformity

316 If past history was all there was to the game, the richest people would be librarians.
— Warren Buffert,
Washington Post, April 17, 1988

317 "Queuemania" is an ailment that afflicts people with a compulsive urge to line up behind someone or something, even a lamp-post.
— Thomas P. Ronan,
New York Times,
Aug. 23, 1955

318 Were it not for the non-conformists, he who refuses to be satisfied to go along with the continuance of things as they are, and insists upon attempting to find new ways of bettering things, the world would have known little progress indeed.
— Josiah William Gitt,
York, *Pennsylvania Gazette and Daily,* Feb. 2, 1957

319 Originality begets conformity.
— Tim Parker,
Omni, May, 1979

320 Conformity is the jailer of freedom and the enemy of growth.
— John F. Kennedy,
address, Sept. 25, 1961

321 Play the revolutionary and challenge the rules — especially the ones you use to govern your day-to-day activities.
— Roger von Oech,
A Whack on the Side of the Head, 1983, ch. 3

322 A man who does not think for himself does not think at all.
— Oscar Wilde,
Oscariana, 1911

323 Most men are individuals no longer as far as their business, its activities, or its moralities are concerned. They are not units but fractions.
— Woodrow Wilson,
speech, Aug. 31, 1910

324 What we call "morals" is simply blind obedience to words of command.
— Havelock Ellis,
The Dance of Life,
1923, ch. 6

325 No one can possibly achieve any real and lasting success or get rich in business by being a conformist.
— J. Paul Getty, *International Herald Tribune,*
Jan. 10, 1961

326 Conform and be dull.
— James Frank Dobie,
The Voice of the Coyote,
1949, introduction

327 When we all think alike, no one is thinking.
— Walter Lippmann,
Poughkeepsie Journal,
March 26, 1978

328 Never forget that only dead fish swim with the stream.
— Malcolm Muggeridge,
quoted by Robert W. Kent,
Money Talks, 1985,
"Managers"

Conscience

329 If you're willing to spend the money and criminality doesn't bother you, you can pretty much buy anything you want.
— August Bequai,
Newsweek, May 2, 1988

330 Suspicion always haunts the guilty mind;
The thief doth fear each bush an officer.
— William Shakespeare,
Henry VI, Part III, 1591,
act V, scene vi, line 11

331 Based on years of study and practice, I have to confess that I find guilt to be much more than a simple tactic. I consider it to be the emotional gravity of the universe. And to those of you who say it's painful, destructive, and unnecessary, all I can say is, "Shame on you!"
— Nicholas V. Iuppa,
Management by Guilt, 1985, part 1

332 I always take blushing either for a sign of guilt, or of ill breeding.
— William Congreve,
The Way of the World,
1700, act I, scene ix

333 Conscience has no more to do with gallantry than it has to do with politics.
— Richard Brinsley Sheridan,
The Duenna, 1775,
act II, scene iv

334 Never do anything against conscience even if the state demands it.
— Albert Einstein,
Saturday Review,
April 30, 1955

335 A good conscience is the best divinity.
— Thomas Fuller,
Gnomologia,
1732, no. 141

336 Conscience is God's presence in man.
— Emanuel Swedenborg,
Arcana Coelestia,
1856, volume 1

337 O conscience, upright and stainless, how bitter a sting to thee is a little fault!
— Dante, *The Divine Comedy,*
ca. 1315, "Purgatory,"
canto III, line 8

338 There is one thing alone that stands the brunt of life throughout its course: a quiet conscience.
— Euripides,
Hippolytus,
428 B.C., line 426

339 There's just ae thing I cannae bear
An' that's my conscience.
— Robert Louis Stevenson,
Underwoods, 1887,
book II,
"In Scots My Conscience"

340 Most people sell their souls and live with a good conscience on the proceeds.
— Logan Pearsall Smith,
Afterthoughts, 1931

Consistency

341 Man is an embodied paradox, a bundle of contradictions.
— Charles Caleb Colton,
Lacon, 1820,
volume I, no. 408

342 You cannot consistently perform in a manner which is inconsistent with the way you see yourself.
— Zig Ziglar,
Top Performance,
1982, ch. 5

343 We are never more true to ourselves than when we are inconsistent.
— Oscar Wilde,
Intentions, 1891

344 A foolish consistency is the hobgoblin of little minds, adored by little statesmen and philosophers and divines. With consistency a great soul has simply nothing to do. He may as well concern himself with his shadow on the wall.
— Ralph Waldo Emerson,
Essays: First Series,
1841, "Self-Reliance"

345 Little things affect little minds.
— Benjamin Disraeli,
Sybil, 1845,
book III, ch. 2

346 Consistency requires you to be as ignorant today as you were a year ago.
— Bernard Berenson,
Notebook, 1892

347 Don't persist in a losing cause unless you truly know you can turn it into a winning one.
— Robert Heller,
The Super Managers,
1984, ch. 2

348 Don't vacillate. A poor plan persevered in is better than a good one shifted while being performed.
— Edwin H. Schell,
quoted by Robert W. Kent,
Money Talks, 1985,
"Managers"

349 There is no more miserable human being than one in whom nothing is habitual but indecision.
— William James,
The Principles of Psychology,
1890, ch. 4

350 Be not careless in deeds, nor confused in words, nor rambling in thought.
— Marcus Aurelius Antoninus,
Meditations, 2nd century A.D.,
book VIII, no. 51

351 How long halt ye between two opinions?
— Bible, I Kings 18:21

352 Indecision has often given an advantage to the other fellow because he did his thinking beforehand.
— Maurice Switzer, quoted by Peter Potter, *All About Success,* 1988, "Goals"

353 We would, and we would not.
— William Shakespeare, *Measure for Measure,* 1605, act IV, scene iv, line 37

Consultants

354 A consultant is someone who takes your watch away to tell you what time it is.
— Ed Finkelstein, *New York Times,* April 29, 1979

355 Because consultants are outsiders, and they don't know the corporate culture, they can ask the dumb questions that no one else would dare ask.
— Tom Ahern, *Computer Decisions* Magazine, July, 1984

356 Consultants are like therapists, after all, and there are some patients who never get out of therapy.
— Sudha M. Pennathur, *Computer Decisions* Magazine, July, 1984

357 As a consultant, you can play political games with great freedom, while maintaining your integrity. You're a lame duck.
— Tom Ahern, *Computer Decisions* Magazine, July, 1984

358 If you need a consultant to tell you what to do or how to find out, then *you're* the problem.
— Robert Townsend, *Further Up the Organization,* 1984, "Consultants: Real Managers Don't Need Them"

Control

359 *Get it all together, v. phr.* 1. to be in full possession and control of one's mental faculties; have a clear purpose well pursued. 2. Retaining one's self-composure under pressure.
— Maxine Tull Boatner, J. Edward Gates, and Adam Makkai, *A Dictionary of American Idioms,* 1987

360 He who doesn't lose his wits over certain things has no wits to lose.
— Gotthold Ephraim Lessing, *Emilia Golotti,* 1772, act IV, scene vii

361 In every organization there are limits on the span of control; increasing amounts of power go to decreasing numbers of people. The slopes of the

pyramid become steeper the
higher up you look.
— Judith M. Bardwick,
The Plateauing Trap,
1988, ch. 3

362 I can get no remedy
against this consumption of the
purse: borrowing only lingers
and lingers it out, but the
disease is incurable.
— William Shakespeare,
Henry IV, Part II, 1598,
act I, scene ii, line 267

363 A control system is not
automatic. A well-designed
system with the best procedures
won't work without attention.
People — not paper — make it
work.
— Joel E. Ross and Michael
J. Kami, *Corporate Management in Crisis: Why the
Mighty Fall,* 1973, ch. 12

364 How many managerial
roles are required when standards are explicit? Does the
need for managers increase in
direct proportion to the levels of
abstraction at which standards
are stated?
— Woodrow H. Sears, Jr.,
Back in Working Order,
1984, ch. 3

365 He that would govern
others, first should be
The master of himself.
— Philip Massinger,
The Bondman,
1624, act I, scene iii

366 The desire to control is
powerful, and when it results in
a listening block, two monologues replace one dialogue.
Two monologues eventually
equal no job.
— Jeffrey G. Allen,
Surviving Corporate Downsizing,
1988, ch. 1

367 Circumstances rule
men; men do not rule circumstances.
— Herodotus,
The History, ca. 450 B.C.,
book VII, ch. 49

Creativity

368 The yellow pad is the
blank canvas of the businessman.
— Bill Ghormley, quoted
by Roger von Oech,
*A Whack on the Side
of the Head,* 1983, "Breaktime"

369 In the office of Rear Ad-
miral Grace Murray Hopper
hangs a clock that runs counter-
clockwise. It's her way of re-
minding visitors that just
because something always has
been done a certain way doesn't
mean it can't be done another
way.
— Ethlie Ann Vare and
Greg Ptacek, *Mothers
of Invention,* "From
Eggbeaters to Eggheads"

370 Creativity always dies a quick death in rooms that house conference tables.
— Bruce Herschensohn, *New York Times,* April 2, 1975

371 Those who create are rare; those who cannot are numerous. Therefore, the latter are stronger.
— Gabrielle Chanel, *This Week,* Aug. 20, 1961

372 Discovery consists of looking at the same thing as everyone else and thinking something different.
— Albert Szent-Györgyi, quoted by Roger von Oech, *A Whack on the Side of the Head*, 1983, introduction

373 Spare the innovation and ruin the company.
— Robert Heller, *The Super Managers,* 1984, ch. 8

374 Take advantage of the ambiguity in the world. Look at something and think about what else it might be.
— Roger von Oech, *A Whack on the Side of the Head,* 1983, ch. 5

375 Some painters transform the sun into a yellow spot, others transform a yellow spot into the sun.
— Pablo Picasso, quoted by Roger von Oech, *A Kick in the Seat of the Pants,* 1986, "The Artist"

376 Creative thinking may simply mean the realization that there's no particular virtue in doing things the way they have always been done.
— Rudolph Flesch, quoted by Roger von Oech, *A Kick in the Seat of the Pants,* 1986, "The Artist"

377 Reading is a means of thinking with another person's mind: It forces you to stretch your own.
— Charles Scribner, Jr., *Publisher's Weekly,* March 30, 1984

378 Absence of occupation is not rest,
A mind quite vacant is a mind distressed.
— William Cowper, *Retirement,* 1782, line 623

379 A hunch is creativity trying to tell you something.
— Frank Capra, quoted by Peter Potter, *All About Success,* 1988, "Creativity"

Criticism

380 *Aristarchian, adj.* extremely critical (from *Aristarch,*

who didn't care for Homer's poetry).
—Josefa Heifetz Byrne,
Mrs. Byrne's Dictionary, 1974

381 People ask you for criticism, but they only want praise.
—William Somerset Maugham,
Of Human Bondage,
1915, ch. 50

382 As far as criticism is concerned, we don't resent that unless it is absolutely biased, as it is in most cases.
—John Vorster,
The Observer, Nov. 9, 1969

383 As to advice, be wary: if it is honest, it is also criticism.
—David Grayson,
quoted by Peter Potter,
All About Success, 1988,
"Advice"

384 If you're not being critical about your business and yourself, you should be.
—Robert Heller,
The Super Managers,
1984, ch. 6

385 The best defensive strategy is the courage to attack yourself.
—Al Ries and Jack Trout,
Marketing Warfare,
1986, ch. 7

386 No man can justly censure or condemn another,

because indeed no man truly knows another.
—Thomas Browne,
Religio Medici,
1643, section IV

387 For I am nothing if not critical.
—William Shakespeare,
Othello, 1605,
act II, scene i, line 119

388 We need very strong ears to hear ourselves judged frankly, and because there are few who can endure frank criticism without being stung by it, those who venture to criticize us perform a remarkable act of friendship, for to undertake to wound or offend a man for his own good is to have a healthy love for him.
—Michel Eyquem de
Montaigne, *Essays,*
1580–1595, book III, ch. 13

389 Do not forget little kindnesses and do not remember small faults.
—Chinese proverb

390 I do not resent criticism, even when, for the sake of emphasis, it parts for the time with reality.
—Winston S. Churchill,
speech, House of Commons,
Jan. 22, 1941

391 Between the barbarity of capitalism, which censures itself

much of the time, and the barbarity of socialism, which does not, I guess I might choose capitalism.
— Bernard-Henri Levy,
Time, March 13, 1978

392 The dread of censure is the death of genius.
— William G. Simms, quoted by Peter Potter, *All About Success*, 1988, "Criticism"

Deception

393 *Cover-up, n., slang* a plan or excuse to escape blame or punishment; lie; alibi.
— Maxine Tull Boatner,
J. Edward Gates, and
Adam Makkai, *A Dictionary of American Idioms*, 1987

394 You can fool all the people all of the time if the advertising is right and the budget is big enough.
— Joseph E. Levine, quoted by Robert W. Kent,
Money Talks, 1985,
"Entrepreneurs"

395 It's the rare test that can't be beaten.
— Robert Half,
Robert Half on Hiring,
1985, ch. 5

396 Men have been swindled by other men on many occasions. The autumn of 1929 was,

perhaps, the first occasion when men succeeded on a large scale in swindling themselves.
— John Kenneth Galbraith,
The Great Crash, 1929,
1955, ch. 7

397 The easiest person to deceive is one's self.
— Edward Bulwer-Lytton,
The Disowned,
1828, ch. 42

398 Nothing is so easy as to deceive one's self; for what we wish, we readily believe.
— Demosthenes,
Third Olynthiac,
349 B.C., section 19

399 Full of wiles, full of guiles, at all times in all ways, are the children of Men.
— Aristophanes, *The Birds,*
ca. 415 B.C., line 451

400 Everything that deceives may be said to enchant.
— Plato, *The Republic,*
ca. 370 B.C., book III,
section 413

401 It is double pleasure to deceive the deceiver.
— Jean de la Fontaine,
Fables, book II,
1668, fable 15

402 The most distrusting persons are often the greatest dupes.
— Paul de Gondi,
Memoirs, 1665, book II

403 There is no benefit in the gifts of a bad man.
—Euripides, *Medea,*
431 B.C., line 618

Decisions

404 Somebody's got to be the guardian of the long term.
—Marina V.N. Whitman,
Forbes, April 4, 1988

405 Whenever you see a successful business, someone once made a courageous decision.
—Peter F. Drucker, quoted by Robert W. Kent, *Money Talks,* 1985, "Managers"

406 The executive exists to make sensible exceptions to general rules.
—Elting E. Morison, quoted by Robert W. Kent, *Money Talks,* 1985, "Managers"

407 Decision makers are those who have the greatest vested interest in the decision.
—Virginia Felix,
Omni, May, 1979

408 The business executive is by profession a decision maker. Uncertainty is his opponent. Overcoming it is his mission. Whether the outcome is a consequence of luck or of wisdom, the moment of decision is without doubt the most creative and critical event in the life of the executive.
—John D. McDonald,
Fortune, Aug., 1955

409 The ability to arrive at complex decisions is the hallmark of the educated person.
—Jean Mayer,
People Weekly,
Nov. 15, 1976

410 Anybody who makes a real decision after 4:00 in the afternoon should have his head examined.
—George C. Marshall,
Book Digest,
June, 1978

411 The absence of alternatives clears the mind marvelously.
—Henry A. Kissinger,
quoted by Peter Potter,
All About Success,
1988, "Decisions"

412 It's easy to make good decisions when there are no bad options.
—Robert Half,
Robert Half on Hiring,
1985, ch. 1

413 Men generally decide upon a middle course . . . for

they know neither how to be entirely good nor entirely bad.
— Niccolò Machiavelli, *Discourses on the First Ten Books of Titus Livius,* 1513–1517, book I, ch. 26

414 Decision making isn't a matter of arriving at a right or wrong answer, it's a matter of selecting the most effective course of action from among less effective courses of action.
— Philip Marvin, *Developing Decisions for Action,* 1971, ch. 6

415 Deliberation is the work of many men. Action, of one alone.
— Charles de Gaulle, quoted by Robert W. Kent, *Money Talks,* 1985, "Managers"

416 In a doubtful case the gentler course is to be pursued.
— The Universal Self-Instructor, 1883, "Legal Maxims"

417 Doubt is not a pleasant condition, but certainty is absurd.
— Voltaire, letter, Nov. 28, 1770

418 If a man will begin with certainties, he shall end in doubts; but if he will be content to begin with doubts, he shall end in certainties.
— Francis Bacon, *Advancement of Learning,* 1605, book I, ch. v, paragraph 8

419 Selling a decision is as important as making a decision. Decision makers must take time to develop selling strategies that turn ideas into action.
— Philip Marvin, *Developing Decisions for Action,* 1971, ch. 15

420 The best way to get a prospect to make a favorable new decision is to make him happy with an old decision.
— Zig Ziglar, *Secrets of Closing the Sale,* 1984, ch. 18

421 There is a time for engagement and a time for withdrawal. A time to walk around the job. A time to con-template it — and a time to just laugh at it.
— Robert Townsend, *Further Up the Organization,* 1984, "Indirection: Don't Neglect It"

422 Never ignore a gut feel-ing: but never believe that it's enough on its own.
— Robert Heller, *The Super Managers,* 1984, ch. 2

423 Let the counsel of thine own heart stand.
— Bible, Apocrypha, Ecclesiasticus 37:13

424 Guess if you can, choose if you dare.
— Pierre Corneille, *Héraclius,* 1646, act IV, scene iv

425 In the multitude of counsellors there is safety.
— Bible, Proverbs 11:14

426 A man that cannot sit still . . . and cannot say no . . . is not fit for business.
— Samuel Pepys, *Diary,* Aug., 1662

427 The plain fact is that there are no conclusions.
— James H. Jeans, *Physics and Philosophy,* 1942

Delegation

428 *Pass the buck, v. phr.* to make another person decide something or accept a responsibility or give orders instead of doing it yourself; shift or escape responsibility or blame; put the duty or blame on someone else.
— Maxine Tull Boatner, J. Edward Gates and Adam Makkai, *A Dictionary of American Idioms,* 1987

429 Nothing is impossible for the man who doesn't have to do it himself.
— A.H. Weiler, *New York Times,* March 17, 1968

430 The female cuckoo can't be bothered to sit on her own eggs. She sneaks them into the nests of other birds, substituting her eggs for theirs, which she tosses out.
— Jane Goodsell, *Not a Good Word About Anybody,* 1988, "Other Children's Parents"

431 The best executive is the one who has sense enough to pick good men to do what he wants done, and self-restraint enough to keep from meddling with them while they do it.
— Theodore Roosevelt, quoted by Robert W. Kent, *Money Talks,* 1985, "Managers"

432 If you want to practice participative management (a good idea), don't fake it — subordinates can spot it, and you.
— Joel E. Ross and Michael J. Kami, *Corporate Management in Crisis: Why the Mighty Fall,* 1973, ch. 4

433 Although the manager assigns part of his responsibilities to other people, he cannot relinquish accountability. Failure cannot be blamed on subordinates. The manager must be in control at all times.
— Ronald Brown, *The Practical Manager's Guide to Excellence in Management,* 1979, ch. 6

434 Not to use is to abuse. If you don't believe this, ask some of your underutilized subordinates.
— William C. Waddell, *Overcoming Murphy's Law,* 1981, ch. 2

435 Identify your highest skill and devote your time to performing it. Delegate all other skills.
— Ronald Brown, *The Practical Manager's Guide to Excellence in Management,* 1979, ch. 1

436 You can delegate authority, but you can never delegate responsibility for delegating a task to someone else. If you picked the right man, fine, but if you picked the wrong man, the responsibility is yours — not his.
— Richard E. Krafve, *Boston Sunday Globe,* May 22, 1960

437 The only people who thoroughly enjoy being assistants-to are vampires.
— Robert Townsend, *Further Up the Organization,* 1984, "Assistants-To and Make-Working"

Discipline

438 *Scaphism, n.* an old Persian method of executing criminals by covering them with honey and letting the sun and the insects finish the job.
— Josefa Heifetz Byrne, *Mrs. Byrne's Dictionary,* 1974

439 It is much safer to obey than to rule.
— Thomas Kempis, *De Imitatione Christi,* ca. 1427, book I, ch. 19

440 When you punish someone, you pay for it later. There was a time when pickpockets were publicly hanged, but other pickpockets took advantage of the large crowds attracted to the executions to ply their trade.
— J. Hopps Barker, *McCall's,* May, 1965

441 In nature there are no rewards or punishments; there are consequences.
— Horace A. Vachell, quoted by Robert W. Kent, *Money Talks,* 1985, "Bottom Line"

442 Hundreds of millions of dollars are spent annually "communicating" with employees. The message always boils down to: "Work hard, obey order. We'll take care of you." (That message is obsolete by fifty years and wasn't very promising then.)
— Robert Townsend, *Further Up the Organization,* 1984, "People"

443 Pardon one offense, and you encourage the commission of many.
— Publilius Syrus, *Maxims,* 1st century B.C., no. 750

444 Permissiveness is only neglect of duty.
— Zig Ziglar, *Top Performance,* 1982, ch. 8

445 Distrust all in whom the impulse to punish is powerful.
— Friedrich Nietzsche,
Thus Spake Zarathustra,
1891, part II, ch. 29

446 It is much safer to be feared than to be loved, when you have to choose between the two.
— Niccolò Machiavelli,
The Prince, 1513, ch. 17

447 If you *have* to have a policy manual, publish the Ten Commandments.
— Robert Townsend,
Further Up the Organization,
1984, "Policy Manuals"

Duty

448 The first duty in life is to be as artificial as possible. What the second duty is no one has yet discovered.
— Oscar Wilde, *Phrases and*
Philosophies for the Use
of the Young, 1891

449 When a stupid man is doing something he is ashamed of, he always decides it is his duty.
— George Bernard Shaw,
Los Angeles Times,
April 30, 1978

450 A sense of duty is moral glue, constantly subject to stress.
— William Safire,
New York Times,
May 23, 1986

451 In practice, it is seldom very hard to do one's duty when one knows what it is, but it is sometimes exceedingly difficult to find this out.
— Samuel Butler,
Kansas City Star,
Oct. 10, 1976

452 When duty calls, that is when character counts.
— William Safire,
New York Times,
May 23, 1986

453 It is rare for businessmen to look upon their civic duties as important.
— Harold Laski, quoted
by Robert W. Kent,
Money Talks, 1985,
"Business Is and Business As"

454 The better part of valor is discretion.
— William Shakespeare,
Henry IV, Part I, 1598,
act V, scene iv, line 120

Economics and Economists

455 Treasury Bill: an ominously worded demand for payment issued by the U.S. Treasury.
— Kurt Brouwer,
Unusual Investment
Definitions, 1987

456 Most of the economics as taught is a form of brain damage.
— Ernst F. Schumacher,
The Reader,
March 25, 1977

457 Money does not pay for anything, never has, never will. It is an economic axiom as old as the hills that goods and services can be paid for only with goods and services.
— Albert Jay Nock,
Memoirs of a Superfluous Man,
1943, part III, ch. 13

458 It's a recession when your neighbor loses his job; it's a depression when you lose your own.
— Harry S Truman,
The Observer,
April 6, 1958

459 We have always known that heedless self-interest was bad morals; we know now that it is bad economics.
— Franklin D. Roosevelt,
second Inaugural Address,
Jan. 20, 1937

460 If ignorance paid dividends, most Americans could make a fortune out of what they don't know about economics.
— Luther Hodges,
Wall Street Journal,
March 14, 1962

461 People want economy and they will pay any price to get it.
— Lee Iacocca,
New York Times,
Oct. 13, 1974

462 The art of taxation consists in so plucking the goose as to obtain the largest possible amount of feathers with the smallest possible amount of hissing.
— Jean Baptiste Colbert,
Time, April 17, 1978

463 As the economy gets better, everything else gets worse.
— Art Buchwald,
Time, Jan. 31, 1972

464 The instability of the economy is equaled only by the instability of economists.
— John Henry Williams,
New York Times,
June 2, 1956

465 If economists were any good at business, they would be rich men instead of advisers to rich men.
— Kirk Kerkorian, quoted
by Robert W. Kent, *Money Talks,* 1985, "Bottom Line"

466 Economists predict gloom because they focus on industrial companies; that's like

predicting a family's future by watching only the grandparents.
—John Naisbitt,
Megatrends,
1984, ch. 3

467 In all recorded history there has not been one economist who had to worry about where the next meal was coming from.
—Peter F. Drucker,
New York Times,
May 16, 1976

468 If all economists were laid end to end, they would not reach a conclusion.
—George Bernard Shaw
(attributed)

Education

469 Education is what survives when what has been learnt has been forgotten.
—B.F. Skinner,
New Scientist,
May 21, 1964

470 If you think education is expensive, try ignorance.
—Derek Bok,
Poughkeepsie Journal,
March 26, 1978

471 It is only the ignorant who despise education.
—Publilius Syrus, *Maxims,*
1st century B.C., no. 571

472 There is nothing as stupid as an educated man if you get him off the thing he was educated in.
—Will Rogers, quoted by Richard M. Ketchum, *Will Rogers, His Life and Times,*
1973, page 401

473 Only the educated are free.
—Epictetus,
Discourses,
ca. 100, book II, ch. 1

474 Education cannot stop with the granting of a diploma. It is, rather, a lifelong process. The manager must learn on the job, translate what he learns into practice, and must free himself from automatic adherence to "the way we have always done it."
—M.J. Rathbone,
Atlanta Economic Review,
April, 1967

475 The direction in which education starts a man, will determine his future life.
—Plato, *The Republic,*
ca. 370 B.C., book IV,
section 425

476 In an information society, education is no mere amenity; it is the prime tool for growing people and profits.
—John Naisbitt and Patricia Aburdene, *Re-inventing the Corporation,* 1985, ch. 5

477 The first quality of a good education is good manners—and some people flunk the course.
— Hubert H. Humphrey, *Connecticut Sunday Herald,* Jan. 1, 1967

478 The purpose of education is to transmit information from decrepit old men to decrepit young men.
— Kenneth E. Boulding, *Omni,* April, 1980

Ego

479 *Acrocephalic, adj.* pertaining to pointed heads. — *n.* someone with a pointed head.
— Josefa Heifetz Byrne, *Mrs. Byrne's Dictionary,* 1974

480 *Admiration, n.* our polite recognition of another's resemblance to ourselves.
— Ambrose Bierce, *The Devil's Dictionary,* 1906

481 Egotism: the art of seeing in yourself what others cannot see.
— George Higgins, *Suburban People News,* March 2, 1986

482 Egoism is the very essence of a noble soul.
— Friedrich Nietzsche, *Beyond Good and Evil,* 1886, no. 265

483 Egotism is the anesthetic that dulls the pain of stupidity.
— Frank Leahy, *Look,* Jan. 10, 1955

484 Conceit is the finest armour a man can wear.
— Jerome K. Jerome, *The Idle Thoughts of an Idle Fellow,* 1889, "On Being Shy"

485 Conceit is God's gift to little men.
— Bruce Barton, *Coronet,* Sept., 1958

486 As for conceit, what man will do any good who is not conceited? Nobody holds a good opinion of a man who has a low opinion of himself.
— Anthony Trollope, *Orley Farm,* 1862, ch. 22

487 Self-approval is joy accompanied with the idea of one's self as the cause.
— Baruch Spinoza, *Ethics,* 1677, book III, proposition 51

488 They are proud in humility; proud that they are not proud.
— Robert Burton, *The Anatomy of Melancholy,* 1651, part I, section 2, member 3, subsection 14

489 Nothing so soothes our vanity as a display of greater vanity in others; it makes us vain, in fact, of our modesty.
— Louis Kronenberger,
Vogue, March 1, 1964

490 The greater thou art, the more humble thyself.
— Bible: Apocrypha,
Ecclesiasticus 3:18

491 The trouble with true humility is, you can't talk about it.
— Michael C. Thomsett,
A Treasury of Business Quotations,
1990, page 46

492 The most difficult secret for a man to keep is the opinion he has of himself.
— Marcel Pagnol,
Reader's Digest,
Oct., 1975

493 Pride . . . is that joy which arises from a man's thinking too much of himself.
— Baruch Spinoza,
Ethics, 1677,
part III, proposition 26

494 Before you tell someone how good you are, you must first tell him how bad you used to be.
— Semon E. Knudsen,
Time, May 25, 1959

495 For God utterly abhors the boasts of a proud tongue.
— Sophocles, *Antigone,*
ca. 440 B.C., line 123

496 Honor modesty more than your life.
— Aeschylus,
The Suppliant Maidens,
ca. 490 B.C., line 1012

497 Good sense is of all things in the world the most equally distributed, for everybody thinks himself so abundantly provided with it, that even those most difficult to please in all other matters do not commonly desire more of it than they already possess.
— René Descartes,
Discourse on the Method,
1637, part I

498 Egoists always have the last word. Once and for all they establish the fact that their minds cannot be changed.
— Marcel Proust,
Remembrance of Things Past,
1913–1926, volume II,
"Within a Budding Grove"

499 Self-made men are most always apt to be a little too proud of the job.
— Henry Wheeler Shaw,
quoted by Robert W. Kent,
Money Talks, 1985,
"Entrepreneurs"

500 Few companies would have reached the going-concern stage without the inflated confidence of their founders. Entrepreneurs tend to be like eighteen-year-old marines who believe the bullet will go right through them without hurt or harm.
— Deaver Brown,
The Entrepreneur's Guide,
1980, ch. 1

501 A man's pride shall bring him low; but honor shall uphold the humble in spirit.
— Bible, Proverbs 29:23

502 The worst disease which can afflict business executives in their work is not, as popularly supposed, alcoholism; it's egotism.
— Harold Geneen with
Alvin Moscow, *Managing,*
1984, ch. 8

503 Every man at his best state is altogether vanity.
— Bible, Psalm 39:5

504 Intellectual arrogance is one form of vanity. There is another form in which the big thing is not self-approval but the need for the approval of others.
— Henry O. Golightly,
Managing with Style,
1977, ch. 3

505 Any man who thinks civilization has advanced is an egoist.
— Will Rogers,
Time, Oct. 7, 1974

Employee Relations

506 *Coffle, n.* a caravan of slaves or cattle chained together.
— Josefa Heifetz Byrne,
Mrs. Byrne's Dictionary, 1974

507 Servitude degrades people to such a point that they come to like it.
— Luc de Clapiers,
*Reflections and
Maxims,* ca. 1747

508 Entrepreneurship is the last refuge of the trouble-making individual.
James K. Glassman,
Washington Monthly,
Oct., 1976

509 The best person you interview isn't necessarily the best person for the job.
— Robert Half,
Robert Half on Hiring,
1985, ch. 10

510 Better fare hard with good men than feast it with bad.
— Thomas Fuller,
Gnomologia,
1732, no. 893

511 The best looking resume may come from the candidate who hires the best resume writer or from the candidate who simply has the most experience writing resumes.
— Robert Half,
Digest of Financial Planning Ideas, July, 1984,
"How to Hire Smart"

512 To keep an organization young and fit, don't hire anyone until everybody's so overworked they'll be glad to see the newcomer no matter where he sits.
— Robert Townsend,
Further Up the Organization,
1984, "No-No's"

513 Caste and class are real issues in organizations, as they are in the rest of society. But in the confined spaces of a plant or corporate headquarters, it is amazing that so much social distance can exist.
— Woodrow H. Sears, Jr.,
Back in Working Order,
1984, ch. 4

514 Remember that when an employee enters your office he is in a strange land.
— Erwin H. Schell,
quoted by Robert W. Kent,
Money Talks, 1985,
"Managers"

515 Supervisor-subordinate relationships are undoubtedly among the oddest forms of human interaction. They are even stranger than kiwi birds at mating time.
— Jeffrey G. Allen,
Surviving Corporate Downsizing,
1988, ch. 3

516 Just being available and attentive is a great way to use listening as a management tool. Some employees will come in, talk for twenty minutes, and leave having solved their problem entirely by themselves.
— Nicholas V. Iuppa,
Management by Guilt,
1985, part 2

517 Surround yourself with the highest caliber people. Remember that first rate people hire first rate people — while second rate people hire third rate people.
— Richard M. White, Jr.,
The Entrepreneur's Manual,
1977, ch. 1

518 The fair request ought to be followed by the deed, in silence.
— Dante, *The Divine Comedy,*
ca. 1315, "Inferno,"
canto XXIV, line 77

519 A strong culture is a system of informal rules that spells out how people are to behave most of the time.
— Terrence E. Deal and
Allen A. Kennedy,
Corporate Cultures, 1982, ch. 1

520 It is a very hard under-taking to seek to please everybody.
— Publilius Syrus, *Maxims,* 1st century B.C., no. 675

521 Anyone who says he isn't going to resign, four times, definitely will.
— John Kenneth Galbraith, *Town and Country,* May, 1979

522 If you don't give your employer a reason to keep you around, don't plan to stay. Working is a value-for-value relationship.
— Jeffrey G. Allen, *Surviving Corporate Downsizing,* 1988, ch. 14

523 A good manager is a man who isn't worried about his own career but rather the careers of those who work for him. My advice: Don't worry about yourself. Take care of those who work for you and you'll float to greatness on their achievements.
— H.S.M. Burns, quoted by Robert W. Kent, *Money Talks,* 1985, "Managers"

524 If I can make an employee happy by spending $800 on a comfortable office chair, what's $800?
— James R. Uffelman, *Wall Street Journal,* Aug. 21, 1984

525 You might be on-line, bug-free, upgraded, converted, and plugged in. But what good is it if your back is killing you?
— Michael C. Thomsett, *A Treasury of Business Quotations,* 1990, page 49

526 It's amazing how many people ruin their backs by sit-ting endlessly at their $3,000 computer in a $3 chair.
— John Bear, *Computer Wimp,* 1983, ch. 2

527 It's not what you pay a man but what he costs you that counts.
— Will Rogers, quoted by Richard M. Ketchum, *Will Rogers, His Life and Times,* 1973, page 401

528 The entrepreneur is similar to a tropical flower that would not survive in a cool, professional corporate environ-ment.
— Deaver Brown, *The Entrepreneur's Guide,* 1980, ch. 1

529 So much of what we call management consists in making it difficult for people to work.
— Peter F. Drucker, *New York Times,* May 16, 1976

Enemies

530 If you're going to be a bridge, you've got to be prepared to be walked upon.
— Roy A. West,
Washington Post, May 8, 1988

531 One enemy is too much.
— George Herbert,
Jacula Prudentum,
1651, no. 523

532 Friends may come and go, but enemies accumulate.
— Thomas Jones,
Wall Street Journal, Feb. 20, 1975

533 A man cannot be too careful in the choice of his enemies.
— Oscar Wilde, *The Picture of Dorian Gray,* 1891, ch. 1

534 The truth is forced upon us, very quickly, by a foe.
— Aristophanes,
The Birds, ca. 415 B.C., line 375

535 To make an enemy, do someone a favor.
— James McLaughry,
Wall Street Journal, Feb. 20, 1975

536 Even a paranoid has some real enemies.
— Henry A. Kissinger,
Newsweek, June 13, 1983

537 Better to be disliked than pitied.
— Abba Eban, *New York Magazine,* July 26, 1976

538 He who has not forgiven an enemy has not yet tasted one of the most sublime enjoyments of life.
— Johann Kaspar Lavater,
Aphorisms on Man, 1788

539 I make enemies deliberately. They are the sauce piquante to my dish of life.
— Elsa Maxwell,
New York Journal-American,
Nov. 2, 1963

540 I bring out the worst in my enemies and that's how I get them to defeat themselves.
— Roy M. Cohn,
New York Times,
Aug. 4, 1986

541 The worst sin towards our fellow creatures is not to hate them, but to be indifferent to them: that's the essence of inhumanity.
— George Bernard Shaw,
The Devil's Disciple,
1901, act II

542 There is nothing harder than the softness of indifference.
— Juan Montalvo, *Chapters Forgotten by Cervantes,*
1895, epilogue

543 I regard you with an indifference closely bordering on aversion.
— Robert Louis Stevenson,
The New Arabian Nights,
1882, "The Rajah's Diamond"

544 There is no little enemy.
—Benjamin Franklin,
Poor Richard's Almanac,
Sept., 1733

Enthusiasm

545 Zeal without knowledge
is fire without light.
—Thomas Fuller,
Gnomologia,
1732, no. 6069

546 Enthusiasm is contagious. It's difficult to remain
neutral or indifferent in the
presence of a positive thinker.
—Denis Waitley and
Remi L. Witt, *The Joy
of Working,* 1985,
"Day 3, Attitude"

547 Irrepressible enthusiasm
and the endurance to withstand
setbacks seem to be crucial
entrepreneurial trademarks.
—Deaver Brown,
The Entrepreneur's Guide,
1980, ch. 1

548 Everyone should learn
to do one thing supremely well
because he likes it, and one
thing supremely well because he
detests it.
—B.W.M. Young,
New York Times,
Jan. 12, 1964

549 We act as though comfort and luxury were the chief

requirements of life, when all
that we need to make us really
happy is something to be
enthusiastic about.
—Charles Kingsley,
Reader's Digest,
July, 1966

550 Indifference and apathy
have one name—betrayal.
—Salvatore Quasimodo,
Saturday Review,
Oct. 26, 1963

551 Unless you can find
some sort of loyalty, you cannot
find unity and peace in your
active living.
—Josiah Royce,
The Philosophy of Loyalty,
1907–1908, lecture 1

552 Vigor is found in the
man who has not yet grown
old, and discretion in the man
who is not too young.
—Onasander,
The General, ca. 40,
ch. 1, section 10

553 For every sale you miss
because you're too enthusiastic,
you will miss a hundred because
you're not enthusiastic enough.
—Zig Ziglar, *Secrets
of Closing the Sale,*
1984, ch. 33

554 Nothing great was ever
achieved without enthusiasm.
—Ralph Waldo Emerson,
Essays: First Series,
1841, "Circles"

Envy

555 Envy is a pain of mind that successful men cause their neighbors.
> —Onasander, *The General,*
> ca. 40, ch. 42, paragraph 25

556 There is not a passion so strongly rooted in the human heart as envy.
> —Richard Brinsley Sheridan,
> *The Critic,* 1779,
> act I, scene i

557 Envy is so natural to human kind that it cannot but arise.
> —Herodotus,
> *The History,* ca. 450 B.C.,
> book III, ch. 80

558 Envy is as persistent as memory, as intractable as a head cold.
> —Harry Stein,
> *Esquire,* July, 1980

559 It is the character of very few men to honor without envy a friend who has prospered.
> —Aeschylus,
> *Agamemnon,*
> ca. 460 B.C., line 832

560 The ear of jealousy heareth all things.
> —Bible: Apocrypha, The
> Wisdom of Solomon 1:10

561 So full of artless jealousy is guilt,

It spills itself in fearing to be spilt.
> —William Shakespeare,
> *Hamlet,* 1601,
> act IV, scene v, line 19

562 Nothing sharpens sight like envy.
> —Thomas Fuller,
> *Gnomologia,*
> 1732, no. 3674

563 It is better to be envied than pitied.
> —Herodotus,
> *The History,* ca. 450 B.C.,
> book III, ch. 52

Errors

564 *Positive, adj.* mistaken at the top of one's voice.
> —Ambrose Bierce,
> *The Devil's Dictionary,* 1906

565 Assumption is the mother of screw-up.
> —Angelo Donghia,
> *New York Times,*
> Jan. 20, 1983

566 Great blunders are often made, like large ropes, of a multitude of fibers.
> —Victor Hugo,
> *Les Misérables,* 1862,
> "Cosette," book V, ch. 10

567 The man who makes no mistakes does not usually make anything.
> —Edward John Phelps,
> speech, Jan. 24, 1899

568 If you make an error, use it as a stepping stone to a new idea you might not have otherwise discovered.
— Roger von Oech, *A Whack on the Side of the Head,* 1983, ch. 6

569 It's always smart to learn from your mistakes. It's even smarter to learn from the mistakes of others.
— Hillel Segal and Jesse Berst, *How to Manage Your Small Computer . . . Without Frustration,* 1983, introduction

570 Old custom without truth is but an old error.
— Thomas Fuller, *Gnomologia,* 1732, no. 3710

571 To obtain maximum attention, it's hard to beat a good, big mistake.
— David D. Hewitt, *Reader's Digest,* Dec., 1987

572 The more a mistake contributes to the system's learning and the building of responsibility, the less effort you should take to prevent it.
— William C. Waddell, *Overcoming Murphy's Law,* 1981, ch. 6

573 A stumble may prevent a fall.
— Thomas Fuller, *Gnomologia,* 1732, no. 424

574 It is safer to err on the side of mercy.
— The Universal Self-Instructor, 1883, "Legal Maxims"

575 Nine times out of ten, in the arts as in life, there is actually no truth to be discovered; there is only error to be exposed.
— H.L. Mencken, *Prejudices, Third Series,* 1922, ch. 3

576 None but the well-bred man knows how to confess a fault, or acknowledge himself in an error.
— Benjamin Franklin, *Poor Richard's Almanac,* Nov., 1738

577 The greatest right in the world is the right to be wrong.
— Harry Weinberger, *New York Evening Post,* April 10, 1917

578 All men are liable to error; and most men are, in many points, by passion or interest, under temptation to it.
— John Locke, *An Essay Concerning Human Understanding,* 1690, book IV, ch. 20, section 17

579 Three-fourths of the mistakes a man makes are made

because he does not really know
the things he thinks he knows.
— James Bryce,
quoted by Peter Potter,
All About Success, 1988,
"Self Knowledge"

580 Time and words can't be
recalled.
— Thomas Fuller,
Gnomologia,
1732, no. 5050

581 Regrets are as personal
as fingerprints.
— Margaret Culkin Banning,
Reader's Digest,
Oct., 1958

582 It is one thing to show a
man that he is in error, and
another to put him in possession of truth.
— John Locke, *An Essay
Concerning Human Understanding,*
1690, book IV, ch. 7, section 11

583 To mourn a mischief
that is past and gone
Is the next way to draw new
mischief on.
— William Shakespeare,
Othello, 1605,
act I, scene iii, line 204

584 The majority of hiring
mistakes made each day would
be prevented if the people
responsible for the hiring simply
did a more effective job of
determining exactly what they

were looking for *before* they
started to look.
— Robert Half,
Robert Half on Hiring,
1985, ch. 2

585 Prophecy is the most
gratuitous form of error.
— George Eliot,
Middlemarch,
1872, ch. 10

Ethics

586 Morality is simply the
attitude we adopt toward people
we personally dislike.
— Oscar Wilde,
An Ideal Husband,
1895, act III

587 Morality is the best of
all devices for leading mankind
by the nose.
— Friedrich Nietzsche,
The Anti-Christ,
1888, aphorism 44

588 Morality is the weakness
of the mind.
— Arthur Rimbaud,
Une Saison en Enfer, 1873

589 What is morality in any
given time or place? It is what
the majority then and there
happen to like, and immorality
is what they dislike.
— Alfred North Whitehead,
*Dialogues of Alfred North
Whitehead,* Aug. 30, 1941

590 Heart, instinct, principles.
— Blaise Pascal
Pensées, 1670, no. 281

591 In civilized life, law floats in a sea of ethics.
— Earl Warren,
New York Times,
Nov. 12, 1962

592 Managers don't have to cook the books to manipulate earnings; they often have all the power they need in the leeway built into accounting rules.
— Ford S. Worthy,
Fortune,
June 25, 1984

593 If a person is an economic being and figures out the odds, then there is a very high incentive to cheat. That is, of course, putting aside honor, duty, and patriotism.
Jerome Kurtz,
Wall Street Journal,
April 10, 1984

594 A clever theft was praiseworthy among the Spartans; and it is equally so amongst Christians, provided it be on a sufficiently large scale.
— Herbert Spencer,
Social Statics,
1850, part II, ch. 16

595 The usual trade and commerce is cheating all round by consent.
— Thomas Fuller,
Gnomologia, 1732, no. 4814

596 Property is not theft, but a good deal of theft becomes property.
— Richard H. Tawney,
*Religion and the Rise
of Capitalism,* 1926, ch. 5

597 Ethics is not a branch of economics.
— Yerachmiel Kugel,
St. Louis Post-Dispatch,
July 24, 1977

598 A criminal is a person with predatory instincts who has not sufficient capital to form a corporation.
— Howard Scott,
quoted by Robert W. Kent,
Money Talks, 1985,
"Business Is and Business As"

599 What to some is called liberty is called license in others.
— Quintilian,
Institutio Oratoria,
1st century A.D., book 3

600 As society is now constituted a literal adherence to the moral precepts scattered throughout the Gospels would mean sudden death.
— Alfred North Whitehead,
Adventures of Ideas,
1933, part I, ch. 2

601 No ethic is as ethical as the work ethic.
— John Kenneth Galbraith,
Cosmopolitan, June, 1980

602 People are beginning to see that the first requisite to success in life is to be a good animal.
> — Herbert Spencer,
> *Education,*
> 1861, ch. 2

603 Crime is a logical extension of the sort of behavior that is often considered perfectly respectable in legitimate business.
> — Robert Rice,
> quoted by Robert W. Kent,
> *Money Talks,* 1985,
> "Business Is and Business As"

604 Not everything legal is honorable.
> — The Universal Self-
> Instructor, 1883
> "Legal Maxims"

605 Mark the perfect man, and behold the upright: for the end of that man is peace.
> — Bible, Psalm 37:37

606 Management assumptions plus management attitudes equals management behavior.
> — Zig Ziglar,
> *Top Performance,*
> 1982, ch. 14

607 The greatest of all faults, I should say, is to be conscious of none.
> — Thomas Carlyle, quoted
> by Peter Potter, *All About
> Success,* 1988, "Satisfaction"

608 What is left when honor is lost?
> — Publilius Syrus, *Maxims,*
> 1st century B.C., no. 265

609 I can resist everything except temptation.
> — Oscar Wilde,
> *Lady Windermere's Fan,*
> 1892, act I

610 Resisting temptation is easier when you think you'll probably get another chance later on.
> — Bob Talbert,
> *Reader's Digest,*
> Oct., 1975

Excellence

611 All excellent things are as difficult as they are rare.
> — Baruch Spinoza,
> *Ethics,* 1677,
> part V, proposition 42

612 Perfection, fortunately, is not the only alternative to mediocrity. A more sensible alternative is excellence. Striving for excellence is stimulating and rewarding; striving for perfection — in practically anything — is both neurotic and futile.
> — Edwin C. Bliss,
> *Doing It Now,*
> 1986, "Step 10:
> Manage Your Time"

613 So much are the modes of excellence settled by time and place that men may be heard boasting in one street of that which they would anxiously conceal in another.
—Samuel Johnson, quoted by Roger von Oech, *A Kick in the Seat of the Pants,* 1986, "The Judge"

614 Output, quality, time, cost, and profit—these are the five unforgiving measures of managerial excellence.
—Lester R. Bittel, *The Nine Master Keys of Management,* 1972, ch. 4

615 Heaven has made one man an excellent soldier; of another it has made a dancer or a singer and player on the lyre.
—Homer, *The Iliad,* 550 B.C., book XIII, line 729

616 It take a long time to bring excellence to maturity.
—Publilius Syrus, *Maxims,* 1st century B.C., no. 780

Experience

617 Experience is the name everyone gives to their mistakes.
—Oscar Wilde, *Lady Windermere's Fan,* 1892, act III

618 No man's knowledge here can go beyond his experience.
—John Locke, *An Essay Concerning Human Understanding,* 1690, book II, ch. 1, section 19

619 Enough experience will make you wise.
—James R. Cook, *The Start-Up Entrepreneur,* 1986, ch. 6

620 They say best men are molded out of faults,
And, for the most, become much more the better
For being a little bad.
—William Shakespeare, *Measure for Measure,* 1605, act V, scene i, line 440

621 A strong and well-constituted man digests his experiences (deeds and misdeeds all included) just as he digests his meats, even when he has some tough morsels to swallow.
—Friedrich Nietzsche, *Genealogy of Morals,* 1887, essay 3, aphorism 16

622 Practice is the best of all instructors.
—Publilius Syrus, *Maxims,* 1st century B.C., no. 439

623 Experience keeps a dear school but fools will learn in no other.
—Benjamin Franklin, *Poor Richard's Almanac,* Dec., 1743

624 The first venture for the entrepreneur tends to serve as a learning experience, a euphemistic term for failure. It is similar to a baby tooth — soon enough it will be replaced by a stronger more durable one.
— Deaver Brown,
The Entrepreneur's Guide,
1980, ch. 3

625 I have but one lamp by which my feet are guided, and that is the lamp of experience.
— Patrick Henry, speech,
March 23, 1775

626 What experience and history teach is this — that peoples and governments have never learned anything from history, or acted on principles deduced from it.
— Georg Wilhelm Friedrich Hegel, *Philosophy of History,*
1832, introduction, section ii

627 For just experience tells;
in every soil
That those that think must govern those that toil.
— Oliver Goldsmith,
The Traveller,
1764, line 371

628 In the business world, everyone is paid in two coins: cash and experience. Take the experience first; the cash will come later.
— Harold Geneen with Alvin Moscow, *Managing,*
1984, ch. 3

629 Experience informs us that the first defense of weak minds is to recriminate.
— Samuel Taylor Coleridge,
Biographia Literaria,
1817, ch. 2

630 Experience makes us see an enormous difference between piety and goodness.
— Blaise Pascal,
Pensées, 1670, no. 496

631 Today is yesterday's pupil.
— Thomas Fuller,
Gnomologia, 1732, no. 5153

632 Not to transmit an experience is to betray it.
— Elie Wiesel,
Christian Science Monitor,
Sept. 18, 1979

Explanation

633 I guess there are two schools of thought about this — yours and mine.
— Ernest Gallo,
New York Times,
May 2, 1988

634 To spell out the obvious is often to call it in question.
— Eric Hoffer,
The Passionate State of Mind,
1954, number 220

635 When stupidity is a sufficient explanation, there is no

need to have recourse to any other.
— Mitchell Ulmann,
Wall Street Journal,
Feb. 26, 1976

636 Never explain. Your friends do not need it and your enemies will not believe you anyway.
— Elbert Hubbard,
Kansas City Star,
Oct. 10, 1976

637 Never complain, never explain.
— Henry Ford II,
New York Times,
March 26, 1979

638 Bad excuses are worse than none.
— Thomas Fuller,
Gnomologia,
1732, no. 833

639 A little inaccuracy sometimes saves tons of explanation.
— H.H. Munro, quoted by
Robert Byrne, *The 637
Best Things Anybody Ever
Said,* 1982, no. 367

Facts

640 Facts are seldom facts, but what people think are facts, heavily tinged with assumptions.
— Harold Geneen with
Alvin Moscow, *Managing,*
1984, ch. 13

641 Facts are stubborn things.
— Alain René Lesage,
Gil Blas, 1735,
book X, ch. 1

642 A fact merely marks the point where we have agreed to let investigation cease.
— Bliss Carman,
Atlantic Monthly,
May, 1906

643 Facts speak for themselves.
— Terence,
The Eunuch,
161 B.C., line 659

644 The way to do research is to attack the facts at the point of greatest astonishment.
— Celia Green, quoted
by Robert W. Kent,
Money Talks, 1985,
"Production and Operations"

645 Never be unreceptive to facts, however discouraging, disappointing, or injurious to your personal welfare they may appear to be.
— Erwin W. Schell, quoted
by Robert W. Kent,
Money Talks,
1985, "Managers"

646 Do not become archivists of facts. Try to penetrate to the secret of their

occurrence, persistently search for the laws which govern them.
—Ivan Pavlov, *To the Academic Youth of Russia,* Feb. 27, 1936

647 Comment is free, but facts are sacred.
—C.P. Scott, *Manchester Guardian,* May 6, 1926

648 No facts are to me sacred; none are profane; I simply experiment, an endless seeker with no Past at my back.
—Ralph Waldo Emerson, *Essays: First Series,* 1841, "Circles"

649 Cynics know the answers without having penetrated deeply enough to know the questions. When challenged by mysterious truths, they marshall "facts."
—Marilyn Ferguson, *The Aquarian Conspiracy,* 1980, page 131

650 When the mind withdraws into itself and dispenses with facts it makes only chaos.
—Edith Hamilton, *The Greek Way,* 1930, ch. 2

651 If we do not find anything pleasant, at least we shall find something new.
—Voltaire, *Candide,* 1759, ch. 17

652 We must always remember that market research, no matter how well done, is based on the past. We are always susceptible to discovering a truth whose time has gone.
—Mark A. Johnson, *The Random Walk and Beyond,* 1988, ch. 3

653 As a rule we disbelieve all facts and theories for which we have no use.
—William James, *The Will to Believe,* 1897

654 Facts from paper are not the same as facts from people. The reliability of the people giving you the facts is as important as the facts themselves.
—Harold Geneen with Alvin Moscow, *Managing,* 1984, ch. 13

655 The greatest American superstition is belief in facts.
—Hermann A. Keyserling, *Kansas City Times,* Jan. 25, 1977

656 Nothing is said nowadays that has not been said before.
—Terence, *The Eunuch,* 161 B.C., line 41

657 There are no eternal facts, as there are no absolute truths.
— Friedrich Nietzsche, *Human, All-too-Human,* 1878

Failure

658 *Atychiphobia, n.* fear of failure.
— Josefa Heifetz Byrne, *Mrs. Byrne's Dictionary,* 1974

659 I cannot give you the formula for success, but I can give you the formula for failure, which is: Try to please everybody.
— Herbert B. Swope, address, Dec. 20, 1950

660 We need to teach the highly educated person that it is not a disgrace to fail and that he must analyze every failure to find its cause. He must learn how to fail intelligently, for failing is one of the greatest arts in the world.
— Charles F. Kettering, quoted by Robert W. Kent, *Money Talks,* 1985, "Managers"

661 In the game of life it's a good idea to have a few early losses, which relieves you of the pressure of trying to maintain an undefeated season.
— Bill Vaughan, quoted by Peter Potter, *All About Success,* 1988, "Adversity"

662 Good people are good because they've come to wisdom through failure. We get very little wisdom from success, you know.
— William Saroyan, *New York Journal-American,* Aug. 23, 1961

663 Failure is instructive. The person who really thinks learns quite as much from his failures as from his successes.
— John Dewey, quoted by Robert W. Kent, *Money Talks,* 1985, "Human Resources"

664 Men learn little from success, but much from failure.
— Arabic proverb

665 He who has never failed somewhere, that man cannot be great.
— Herman Melville, *The Literary World,* Aug., 1850

666 Remember there are two benefits of failure. First, if you do fail, you learn what doesn't work; and second, the

failure gives you an opportunity
to try a new approach.
—Roger von Oech,
*A Whack on the Side
of the Head,* 1983, ch. 6

667 It is possible to fail in
many ways . . . while to succeed
is possible only in one way.
—Aristotle,
Nicomachean Ethics,
ca. 330 B.C., book II, ch. 6

668 When you are down and
out, something always turns
up—and it is usually the noses
of your friends.
—Orson Welles,
New York Times,
April 1, 1962

669 The cream rises until it
sours.
—Laurence J. Peter,
San Francisco Chronicle,
Jan. 29, 1978

670 It is better to fail in
originality than to succeed in
imitation.
—Herman Melville,
The Literary World,
Aug., 1850

671 Post-mortems on defeat
are never very useful unless
they say something about the
future.
—James Reston,
New York Times,
July 15, 1964

672 We are all refugees of a
future that never happened.
—Lee Weiner,
People, Sept. 12, 1977

Faith

673 "Faith" means not wanting to know what is true.
—Friedrich Nietzsche,
The Anti-Christ, 1888,
aphorism 8

674 How many things which
served us yesterday as articles of
faith, are fables for us today.
—Michel Eyquem de
Montaigne, *Essays,*
1580–1595, book I, ch. 26

675 Our faith comes in
moments; our vice is habitual.
—Ralph Waldo Emerson,
Essays: First Series,
1841, "The Over-Soul"

676 Faith, fantastic faith
once wedded fast,
To some dear falsehood, hugs it
to the last.
—Thomas Moore,
Lalla Rookh, 1817

677 The faith that stands on
authority is not faith.
—Ralph Waldo Emerson,
Essays: First Series,
1841, "The Over-Soul"

Flattery

678 *Captation, n.* 1. the act of controlling another's mind. 2. trying to cadge acceptance by flattery. 3. formerly, the first stage of a hypnotic trance.
—Josefa Heifetz Byrne,
Mrs. Byrne's Dictionary, 1974

679 To ask advice is in nine cases out of ten to tout for flattery.
—John C. Collins,
Aphorisms, 1901, no. 59

680 There is no way of guarding oneself from flatterers except letting men understand that to tell you the truth does not offend you; but when everyone may tell you the truth, you lose their respect.
—Niccolò Machiavelli,
The Prince, 1513, ch. 23

681 Meddle not with him that flattereth with his lips.
—Bible, Proverbs 20:19

682 There are none who are more taken by flattery than the proud, who wish to be first and are not so.
—Baruch Spinoza,
Ethics, 1677,
part IV, appendix, XXI

683 A flatterer can risk everything with great personages.
—Alain René Lesage,
Gil Blas, 1735,
book IV, ch. 7

684 Among all the diseases of the mind there is not one more epidemical or more pernicious than the love of flattery.
—Richard Steele,
The Spectator,
1711, no. 238

685 More people are flattered into virtue than bullied out of vice.
—R.S. Surtees,
*The Analysis of the
Hunting Field,* 1846, ch. 1

Fools

686 *Boobocracy, n.* government by boobs; plebianism ad absurdum (slang).
—Josefa Heifetz Byrne,
Mrs. Byrne's Dictionary, 1974

687 Only the most foolish of mice would hide in a cat's ear. But only the wisest of cats would think to look there.
—Andrew Mercer, quoted by
Roger von Oech, *A Whack
on the Side of the Head,*
1983, "Breaktime"

688 At times discretion should be thrown aside, and with the foolish we should play the fool.
—Menander,
Those Offered for Sale,
3rd century B.C.,
fragment 421

689 Every man is a divinity in disguise, a god playing the fool.
— Ralph Waldo Emerson,
Essays: First Series,
1841, "Heroism"

690 The way of a fool is right in his own eyes.
— Bible, Proverbs 12:15

691 Let a fool be made serviceable according to his folly.
— Joseph Conrad,
Under Western Eyes,
1911, part I, ch. 3

692 Hain't we got all the fools in town on our side? And ain't that a big enough majority in any town?
— Mark Twain,
Adventures of Huckleberry Finn, 1884, ch. 26

693 I had rather have a fool to make me merry than experience to make me sad.
— William Shakespeare,
As You Like It, 1600,
act IV, scene i, line 28

694 Let a fool hold his tongue and he will pass for a sage.
— Publilius Syrus, *Maxims,*
1st century B.C., no. 914

695 A wise man may look ridiculous in the company of fools.
— Thomas Fuller,
Gnomologia, 1732, no. 474

696 Talk sense to a fool and he calls you foolish.
— Euripides, *The Bacchae,*
ca. 410 B.C., line 480

697 Even a fool may be wise after the event.
— Homer, *The Iliad,*
ca. 550 B.C.,
book XVII, line 32

698 Do you think that the things people make fools of themselves about are any less real and true than the things they behave sensibly about?
— George Bernard Shaw,
Candida, 1898, act I

699 No man really becomes a fool until he stops asking questions.
— Charles P. Steinmetz,
quoted by Peter Potter,
All About Success,
1988, "Curiosity"

Friendship

700 *Good egg,* slang or informal, *good scout, n. phr.* a friendly, kind or good-natured person; a nice fellow.
— Maxine Tull Boatner,
J. Edward Gates, and
Adam Makkai, *A Dictionary of American Idioms,* 1987

701 Help me to money and I'll help myself to friends.
— Thomas Fuller,
Gnomologia, 1732, no. 1030

702 I will not be ashamed to defend a friend.
　　　　—Bible: Apocrypha,
　　　　Ecclesiasticus 22:25

703 No man is useless while he has a friend.
　　　—Robert Louis Stevenson,
　　　　　Across the Plain,
　　　　1892, "Lay Morals"

704 Nature teaches beasts to know their friends.
　　　　—William Shakespeare,
　　　　Coriolanus, 1608, act II,
　　　　　　scene i, line 6

705 Have no friends not equal to yourself.
　　　　—Confucius, *Analects,*
　　　ca. 500 B.C., book I, ch. 8

706 A friend in power is a friend lost.
　　　　—Henry Brooks Adams,
　　　　*The Education of Henry
　　　　　Adams,* 1907, ch. 7

707 I am amazed that anyone who has made a fortune should send for his friends.
　　　　　—Aristophanes,
　　Plutus, ca. 390 B.C., line 340

708 A friend cannot be known in prosperity: and an enemy cannot be hidden in adversity.
　　　　—Bible: Apocrypha,
　　　　Ecclesiasticus 12:8

709 He that wants money, means, and content, is without three good friends.
　　　　—William Shakespeare,
　　　　　As You Like It, 1600,
　　　　act III, scene ii, line 25

710 There are three faithful friends—an old wife, an old dog, and ready money.
　　　　—Benjamin Franklin,
　　　　Poor Richard's Almanac,
　　　　　　Jan., 1738

711 We shall never have friends, if we expect to find them without faults.
　　—Thomas Fuller, *Gnomologia,*
　　　　　1732, no. 5456

712 I do desire we may be better strangers.
　　　　—William Shakespeare,
　　　　　As You Like It, 1600,
　　　　act III, scene ii, line 276

713 He's my friend that speaks well of me behind my back.
　　—Thomas Fuller, *Gnomologia,*
　　　　　1732, no. 2465

Genius

714 Genius [is] little more than the faculty of perceiving in an unhabitual way.
　　　　　—William James,
　　　The Principles of Psychology,
　　　　　　1890, ch. 19

715 Genius is the ability to reduce the complicated to the simple.
— C.W. Ceram, quoted by Peter Potter, *All About Success,* 1988, "Genius"

716 Genius is one of the many forms of insanity.
— Cesare Lombroso, *The Man of Genius,* 1891

717 When a true genius appears in this world you may know him by this sign, that the dunces are all in confederacy against him.
— Jonathan Swift, *Thoughts on Various Subjects,* 1706

718 Genius all over the world stands hand in hand, and one shock of recognition runs the whole circle round.
— Herman Melville, *Hawthorne and His Mosses,* 1850

719 The public is wonderfully tolerant. They forgive everything except genius.
— Oscar Wilde, *Intentions,* 1891

720 Everybody is born with genius, but most people only keep it a few minutes.
— Edgard Varèse, *New York Times,* March 31, 1985

721 The difference between genius and stupidity is that genius has its limits.
— Anonymous

Goals

722 The trouble with our age is all signposts and no destination.
— Louis Kronenberger, *Look,* May 17, 1954

723 The tragedy of life doesn't lie in not reaching your goal. The tragedy lies in having no goal to reach.
— Benjamin E. Mays, *New York Times,* May 16, 1985

724 Very few people are ambitious in the sense of having a specific image of what they want to achieve. Most people's sights are only toward the next run, the next increment of money.
— Judith M. Bardwick, *The Plateauing Trap,* 1988, ch. 4

725 Management by objectives works if you know the objectives. Ninety percent of the time you don't.
— Peter F. Drucker, quoted by Robert W. Kent, *Money Talks,* 1985, "Managers"

726 The test of management is whether or not it achieves the goals it sets for itself; the higher

the goals, the better the management. In fact, if the level of goals is too low, I wouldn't call it management at all; anyone can do it.
— Harold Geneen with
Alvin Moscow, *Managing,*
1984, ch. 13

727 Happiness, wealth, and success are byproducts of goal setting; they cannot be the goal themselves.
— Denis Waitley and
Remi L. Witt, *The Joy
of Working,* 1985,
"Day 5, Goal Setting"

728 Always the rationalization is the same — "Once this situation is remedied, then I will be happy." But it never works that way in reality: The goal is achieved, but the person who reaches it is not the same person who dreamed it. The goal was static, but the person's identity was dynamic.
— Phillip Moffit,
Esquire, Sept., 1984

729 As long as people don't change what is important to them — as long as promotion is the only outcome that counts — many will be frustrated. When people change what they value so they have goals that are both important and achievable, they can be satisfied.
— Judith M. Bardwick,
The Plateauing Trap,
1988, ch. 1

730 American business needs a lifting purpose greater than the struggle of materialism.
— Herbert Hoover,
quoted by Robert W. Kent,
Money Talks, 1985,
"Bottom Line"

731 Every great man of business has got somewhere a touch of the idealist in him.
— Woodrow Wilson,
quoted by Peter Potter,
All About Success,
1988, "Dreams"

732 Those who aim low usually hit their target.
— Denis Waitley and
Remi L. Witt, *The Joy
of Working,* 1985,
"Day 15, Motivation"

733 In the long run men hit only what they aim at.
— Henry David Thoreau,
Walden, 1854,
I, "Economy"

734 Your goal should be just out of reach, but not out of sight.
— Denis Waitley and
Remi L. Witt, *The Joy
of Working,* 1985,
"Day 5, Goal Setting"

735 Slight not what's near through aiming at what's far.
— Euripides, *Rhesus,*
ca. 435 B.C., line 482

736 We are all in the gutter, but some of us are looking at the stars.
— Oscar Wilde,
Lady Windermere's Fan,
1891, act I

737 When you reach for the stars, you may not quite get one, but you won't come up with a handful of mud either.
— Leo Burnett,
Reader's Digest,
Jan., 1985

738 As one approaches any goal, it seems more reasonable that one should reach it, and desire commences to look beyond.
— Richard P. Wilbur,
Washington University Magazine,
Summer, 1964

739 There are two tragedies in life. One is not to get your heart's desire. The other is to get it.
— George Bernard Shaw,
Man and Superman,
1903, act IV

740 The want of a thing is perplexing enough, but the possession of it is intolerable.
— John Vanbrugh,
The Confederacy,
1705, act I, scene ii

741 Being frustrated is disagreeable, but the real disasters of life begin when you get what you want.
— Irving Kristol,
Newsweek,
Nov. 28, 1977

742 If you have built castles in the air, your work need not be lost; that is where they should be. Now put the foundations under them.
— Henry David Thoreau,
quoted by Peter Potter,
All About Success, 1988, "Dreams"

743 Common goals plus a common cause equals greater success.
— Zig Ziglar,
Top Performance,
1982, ch. 2

Gossip

744 Gossip, unlike river water, flows both ways.
— Michael Korda,
Reader's Digest,
June, 1976

745 Keep thy tongue from evil, and thy lips from speaking guile.
— Bible, Psalm 34:13

746 Tale-bearers are as bad as the tale-makers.
— Richard Brinsley Sheridan,
The School for Scandal, 1777,
act I, scene i

747 I set it down as a fact that if all men knew what each said of the other, there would not be four friends in the world.
— Blaise Pascal,
Pensées, 1670, no. 101

748 He multiplieth words without knowledge.
— Bible, Job 35:16

749 Without a steady diet of news about people one knows, life in most companies would be grim — and pretty dull.
— Terrence E. Deal and
Allen A. Kennedy,
Corporate Cultures,
1982, ch. 5

750 In all labor there is profit; but the talk of the lip tendeth only to penury.
— Bible, Proverbs 14:23

751 Do not repeat slander; you should not hear it, for it is the result of hot temper.
— Ptahhotep, *The Maxims of
Ptahhotep,* ca. 2350 B.C.,
maxim 23

752 Thou shalt not go up and down as a talebearer among thy people.
— Bible, Leviticus 19:16

753 There are no secrets better kept than the secrets that everybody guesses.
— George Bernard Shaw,
Mrs. Warren's Profession,
1893, act III

754 What is told in the ear of a man is often heard a hundred miles away.
— Chinese proverb

755 I know that's a secret, for it's whispered everywhere.
— William Congreve,
Love for Love,
1695, act III, scene iii

756 Rumor is a pipe
Blown by surmises, jealousies, conjectures,
And of so easy and so plain to stop
That the blunt monster with uncounted heads
The still-discordant wavering multitude,
Can play upon it.
— William Shakespeare,
Henry IV, Part II
1598, induction, line 15

757 Should a wise man utter vain knowledge and fill his belly with the east wind?
— Bible, Job 15:2

758 Whistler's mother opened other people's mail.
— Jane Goodsell,
Not a Good Word About Anybody,
1988, "Nobody's Perfect"

759 That which is everybody's business is nobody's business.
— Izaak Walton,
quoted by Robert W. Kent,
Money Talks, 1985,
"Business Is and Business As"

760 I cannot hold with those who wish to put down the insignificant chatter of the world.
— Anthony Trollope,
Framley Personage,
1860, ch. 10

761 Many have fallen by the edge of the sword: but not so many as have fallen by the tongue.
— Bible: Apocrypha,
Ecclesiasticus 28:18

762 Gossips are not expected to be serious people; and they are not always expected to get the news right. They are expected simply to entertain.
— Terrence E. Deal
and Allen A. Kennedy,
Corporate Cultures,
1982, ch. 5

763 There is only one thing in the world worse than being talked about, and that is not being talked about.
— Oscar Wilde, *The Picture of Dorian Gray,* 1891, ch. 1

Happiness

764 *Grinagog, n.* a perpetual grinner (slang).
— Josefa Heifetz Byrne,
Mrs. Byrne's Dictionary, 1974

765 We rarely find anyone who can say he has lived a happy life, and who, content with his life, can retire from the world like a satisfied guest.
— Horace, *Satires,*
book I, 35 B.C.,
satire i, line 117

766 Happy the man who could search out the causes of things.
— Virgil, *Georgics II,*
ca. 30 B.C., line 490

767 If happiness is activity in accordance with virtue, it is reasonable that it should be in accordance with the highest virtue.
— Aristotle, *Nicomachean Ethics,*
ca. 330 B.C., book X, ch. 7

768 We have no more right to consume happiness without producing it than to consume wealth without producing it.
— George Bernard Shaw,
Candida, 1898, act I

769 Happiness is not something owed you. Nobody is handed joy on a silver platter. Instead, you make your own happiness, knowing it is an attitude, a habit gained from daily practice.
— Denis Waitley and
Remi L. Witt, *The Joy of Working,* 1985, prologue

770 He is well paid that is well satisfied.
— William Shakespeare,
The Merchant of Venice, 1596,
act IV, scene i, line 416

771 [It is the] rare happiness of times when we may think what we please, and express what we think.
— Cornelius Tacitus,
The Histories,
ca. A.D. 95, book I, ch. 1

772 He who is of a calm and happy nature will hardly feel the pressure of age, but to him who is of an opposite disposition youth and age are equally a burden.
— Plato, *The Republic,*
ca. 370 B.C., book I,
section 329

773 A lifetime of happiness! No man alive could bear it: it would be hell on earth.
— George Bernard Shaw,
Man and Superman,
1903, act I

774 Misery no longer loves company. Nowadays it insists upon it.
— Russell Baker,
Washingtonian,
Nov., 1978

775 Call no man happy, till his contented clay is cold.
— Aeschylus,
Agamemnon,
ca. 460 B.C., line 928

776 No man is happy who does not think himself so.
— Publilius Syrus, *Maxims,*
1st century B.C., no. 584

777 In about the same degree as you are helpful, you will be happy.
— Karl Reiland,
New York Herald Tribune,
Nov. 6, 1961

778 A feast is made for laughter, and wine maketh merry: but money answereth all things.
— Bible, Ecclesiastes 10:19

779 The secret of happiness is to admire without desiring. And that is not happiness.
— F.H. Bradley,
Aphorisms, 1930, no. 33

Haste

780 A hasty man drinks his tea with a fork.
— Chinese proverb

781 Let no man boast himself that he has got through the perils of winter till at least the seventh of May.
— Anthony Trollope,
Doctor Thorne,
1858, ch. 47

782 The haste of a fool is the slowest thing in the world.
— Thomas Shadwell,
A True Widow,
1679, act III, scene i

783 People who act without due consideration of the

business in hand lose even what they have within their grasp.
— Aesop, fable,
"One Thing at a Time,"
ca. 550 B.C.

784 How poor are they that have not patience!
What wound did ever heal but by degrees?
— William Shakespeare,
Othello, 1605,
act II, scene iii, line 379

785 Learn to pause . . . or nothing worthwhile will catch up to you.
— Doug King, quoted by Roger von Oech,
A Kick in the Seat of the Pants,
1986, "The Artist"

786 Haste in every business brings failures.
— Herodotus,
The History, ca. 450 B.C.,
book VII, ch. 10

Honesty

787 *Clean hands, n. phr., slang* freedom from guilt or dishonesty; innocence.
— Maxine Tull Boatner,
J. Edward Gates, and
Adam Makkai, *A Dictionary of American Idioms,* 1987

788 A good reputation is more valuable than money.
— Publilius Syrus, *Maxims,*
1st century B.C., no. 108

789 To be honest, as this world goes, is to be one man picked out of ten thousand.
— William Shakespeare,
Hamlet, 1601,
act II, scene ii, line 179

790 It is difficult but not impossible to conduct strictly honest business. What is true is that honesty is incompatible with the amassing of a large fortune.
— Mohandas K. Gandhi,
quoted by Robert W. Kent,
Money Talks, 1985,
"Business Is and Business As"

791 It is nearly always easier to make $1,000,000 honestly than to dispose of it wisely.
— Julius Rosenwald,
Saturday Review,
Jan. 19, 1968

792 Honesty pays, but it doesn't seem to pay enough to suit some people.
— Frank McKinney Hubbard,
quoted by Robert W. Kent,
Money Talks,
1985, "Bottom Line"

793 The reader deserves an honest opinion. If he doesn't deserve it, give it to him anyhow.
— John Ciardi,
Saturday Review,
Feb. 16, 1957

794 A truth that's told with bad intent

Beats all the lies you can
invent.
— William Blake, *Poems from
the Pickering Manuscript,*
ca. 1805, "Auguries of
Innocence," line 53

795 He that resolves to deal
with none but honest men must
leave off dealing.
— Thomas Fuller,
Gnomologia,
1732, no. 2267

796 Always be ready to
speak your mind and a base
man will avoid you.
— William Blake, quoted
by Peter Potter, *All About
Success,* 1988, "Honesty"

797 Being entirely honest
with oneself is a good exercise.
— Sigmund Freud,
letter, Oct. 15, 1897

798 Never esteem anything
as of advantage to you that will
make you break your word or
lose your self-respect.
— Marcus Aurelius
Antoninus, *Meditations,*
2nd century A.D.,
book III, no. 7

799 If liberty means
anything at all, it means the
right to tell people what they do
not want to hear.
— George Orwell,
Animal Farm, 1945,
introduction

800 Though it be honest, it
is never good
To bring bad news.
— William Shakespeare,
Antony and Cleopatra, 1607,
act II, scene v, line 85

801 A man should be
upright, not be kept upright.
— Marcus Aurelius
Antoninus, *Meditations,*
1st century A.D.,
book III, no. 5

Humor

802 Brevity is the soul of
wit.
— William Shakespeare,
Hamlet, 1601,
act II, scene ii, line 90

803 The banalities of a great
man pass for wit.
— Alexander Chase,
Perspectives, 1966

804 Shall I crack any of
those old jokes at which the
audience never fail to laugh?
— Aristophanes,
The Frogs,
ca. 405 B.C., line 1

805 It's amazing how important humor is considered to be
in this town. The power it has —
what it can do for you and what
it can do against you.
— Landon Parvin, quoted by
Gerald Gardner, *All the
Presidents' Wits,* 1986, ch. 2

806 When men drink, they thrive, grow wealthy, profit, win lawsuits, make themselves happy, help their friends. Go fetch me a bearer of wine, and let me moisten my wits, and utter something clever.
— Aristophanes,
The Knights,
ca. 425 B.C., line 92

807 I shall ne'er be ware of mine own wit, till I break my shins against it.
— William Shakespeare,
As You Like It, 1600,
act II, scene iv, line 59

808 There are three things which are real — God, human folly, and laughter. The first two are beyond our comprehension, so we must do what we can with the third.
— John F. Kennedy, quoted by Gerald Gardner,
All the Presidents' Wits,
1986, introduction

809 You have to have a serious streak in you or you can't see the funny side of the other fellow.
— Will Rogers, quoted by Richard M. Ketchum,
Will Rogers, His Life and Times, 1973, page 191

Hypocrisy

810 Hypocrisy is the homage vice pays to virtue.
— François, Duc de la Rochefoucauld, *Reflections; or, Sentences and Moral Maxims,*
1665, maxim 218

811 No man, for any considerable period, can wear one face to himself, and another to the multitude, without finally getting bewildered as to which may be the true.
— Nathaniel Hawthorne,
The Scarlet Letter,
1850, ch. 20

812 What kind of truth is this which is true on one side of a mountain and false on the other?
— Michel Eyquem de Montaigne, *Essays,* 1580–1595,
book I, ch. 39

813 The only vice that cannot be forgiven is hypocrisy. The repentance of a hypocrite is itself hypocrisy.
— William Hazlitt,
Characteristics,
1823, ch. 22

814   It oft falls out
To have what we would have,
we speak not what we mean.
— William Shakespeare,
Measure for Measure, 1605,
act II, scene iv, line 118

815 Every man alone is sincere. At the entrance of a second person, hypocrisy begins.
— Ralph Waldo Emerson,
Essays: First Series,
1841, "Friendship"

Ideas

816 Public opinion exists only where there are no ideas.
— Oscar Wilde,
Saturday Review,
Nov. 17, 1894

817 Not to engage in the pursuit of ideas is to live like ants instead of like men.
— Mortimer J. Adler,
Saturday Review,
Nov. 22, 1958

818 A new idea is delicate. It can be killed by a sneer or a yawn; it can be stabbed to death by a quip and worried to death by a frown on the right man's brow.
— Charles Brower,
Advertising Age,
Aug. 10, 1959

819 Getting ideas is like shaving: if you don't do it every day, you're a bum.
— Alex Kroll, quoted by
Roger von Oech, *A Kick
in the Seat of the Pants,*
1986, "Jack's Return Visit
to the Idea Doctor"

820 A new and valid idea is worth more than a regiment and fewer men can furnish the former than can command the latter.
— Oliver Wendell Holmes, Jr.,
letter, July 21, 1925

821 It's easy to come up with new ideas; the hard part is letting go of what worked for you two years ago, but will soon be out-of-date.
— Roger von Oech,
*A Kick in the Seat
of the Pants,* 1986, "The Judge"

822 Every time you come up with a terrific idea, you find that someone else thought of it first.
— Frank Harden,
Washingtonian,
Nov., 1978

823 Nothing is more dangerous than an idea when it is the only one you have.
— Émile Chartier, quoted
by Roger von Oech,
*A Whack on the Side of
the Head,* 1983, ch. 1

824 The insolence of authority is endeavoring to substitute money for ideas.
— Frank Lloyd Wright,
A Testament, 1957

825 Develop the hunter's attitude, the outlook that wherever

you go, there are ideas waiting
to be discovered.
— Roger von Oech,
*A Whack on the Side
of the Head,* 1983, ch. 8

826 There is nothing so
powerful as an old idea whose
time has come again.
— Ben Wattenberg,
Washingtonian,
Nov., 1979

827 An idea that is not
dangerous is unworthy to be
called an idea at all.
— Elbert Hubbard,
Dictionary of Epigrams, 1910

828 What we are this day
justifying by precedents, will be
itself a precedent.
— Cornelius Tacitus,
The Annals, ca. A.D. 100,
book XI, ch. 24

829 As soon as an idea is accepted it is time to reject it.
— Holbrook Jackson, quoted
by Robert W. Kent, *Money
Talks,* 1985, "Bottom Line"

830 To die for an idea is to
place a pretty high price upon
conjectures.
— Anatole France,
La Révolte des Anges,
1914, ch. 8

831 To die for an idea; it is
unquestionably noble. But how

much nobler it would be if men
died for ideas that were true!
— H.L. Mencken,
*Prejudices, First
Series,* 1919

832 A fixed idea ends in
madness or heroism.
— Victor Hugo,
Quatre-vingt-treize,
1879, part 2

833 There is an everlasting
struggle in every mind between
the tendency to keep un-
changed, and the tendency to
renovate its ideas.
— William James,
The Principles of Psychology,
1890, ch. 19

834 The hours of a wise
man are lengthened by his
ideas.
— Joseph Addison,
The Spectator,
June 18, 1711

835 Who can refute a sneer?
— William Paley,
*Principles of Moral Philosophy
and Political Philosophy,*
1785, volume II, book V, ch. 9

836 I can't help it. I was
born sneering.
— William S. Gilbert,
The Mikado,
1885, act I

837 An invasion of armies can be resisted; an invasion of ideas cannot be resisted.
— Victor Hugo,
Histoire d'un Crime,
1877, "Le Chute," X

Idleness

838 You must keep people scared every day.
— Peter Grace,
Financial World,
April 5, 1988

839 People who are resting on their laurels are wearing them on the wrong end.
— Malcolm Kushner, quoted by Roger von Oech, *A Kick in the Seat of the Pants,* 1986, "Jack's Visit to the Idea Doctor"

840 There are an enormous number of managers who have retired on the job.
— Peter F. Drucker,
quoted by Peter Potter,
All About Success, 1988,
"Laziness"

841 He has spent all his life in letting down empty buckets into empty wells; and he is frittering away his age in trying to draw them up again.
— Sydney Smith,
Lady Holland's Memoir,
1855, volume I, ch. 9

842 An unused life is an early death.
— Johann Wolfgang von Goethe, *Iphigenie auf Tauris,* 1787, act I, scene i

843 Yearning is not only a good way to go crazy but also a pretty good place to hide out from hard truth.
— Jay Cocks,
Time, Oct., 1984

844 The world is full of willing people: some willing to work, the rest willing to let them.
— Robert Frost, quoted by Robert W. Kent, *Money Talks,* 1985, "Human Resources"

845 Idle men are dead all their life long.
— Thomas Fuller, *Gnomologia,* 1732, no. 3055

846 The hardest job of all is trying to look busy when you're not.
— William Feather, quoted by Robert W. Kent, *Money Talks,* 1985, "Business Is and Business As"

Ignorance

847 One of the greatest pieces of economic wisdom is to know what you do not know.
— John Kenneth Galbraith,
Time, March 3, 1961

848 The recipe for perpetual ignorance is: Be satisfied with your opinions and content with your knowledge.
— Elbert Hubbard, quoted by Peter Potter, *All About Success,* 1988, "Arrogance"

849 Ignorance is not bliss— it is oblivion.
— Philip Wylie, *Generation of Vipers,* 1942

850 Better be ignorant of a matter than half know it.
— Publilius Syrus, *Maxims,* 1st century B.C., no. 865

851 Do not be arrogant because of your knowledge, but confer with the ignorant man as well as with the learned.
— Ptahhotep, *The Maxims of Ptahhotep,* ca. 2350 B.C., maxim no. 1

852 Everybody is ignorant, only on different subjects.
— Will Rogers, quoted by Richard M. Ketchum, *Will Rogers, His Life and Times,* 1973, page 401

853 Blessed are the forgetful; for they get over their stupidities too.
— Friedrich Nietzsche, *Beyond Good and Evil,* 1886, no. 217

854 All you need in this life is ignorance and confidence, and then success is sure.
— Mark Twain, letter, Dec. 2, 1878

855 To know anything well involves a profound sensation of ignorance.
— John Ruskin, *Modern Painters,* 1843, volume I, part I, ch. 3

856 The greatest obstacle to discovery is not ignorance— it is the illusion of knowledge.
— Daniel J. Boorstin, *Washington Post,* Jan. 29, 1984

857 Against stupidity the very gods
Themselves contend in vain.
— Johann Christoph Friedrich von Schiller, *Die Jungfrau von Orleans,* 1801, act III, scene vi

858 It pays to be ignorant, for when you're smart you already know it can't be done.
— Jeno F. Palucci, *New York Times,* Nov. 7, 1976

859 Curiosity is a willing, a proud, an eager confession of ignorance.
— Leonard Rubinstein, *Reader's Digest,* Oct., 1984

860 There is no sin except stupidity.
— Oscar Wilde, *The Critic as Artist*, 1891, part II

861 Half a brain is enough for him who says little.
— Italian proverb

Imagination

862 Trying to define yourself is like trying to bite your own teeth.
— Alan Watts, *Life*, April 21, 1961

863 Imagination was given to man to compensate him for what he is not. A sense of humor was provided to console him for what he is.
— Horace Walpole, quoted by Roger von Oech, *A Kick in the Seat of the Pants*, 1986, "The Artist"

864 The moment a person forms a theory, his imagination sees in every object, only the traits which favor that theory.
— Thomas Jefferson, letter, Sept. 20, 1787

865 The amount a person uses his imagination is inversely proportional to the amount of punishment he will receive for using it.
— Roger von Oech, *A Whack on the Side of the Head*, 1983, ch. 4

866 It would be a great mistake to confine your imagination to the way things have always been done. In fact, it would consign you to the mediocrity of the marketplace.
— Harold Geneen with Alvin Moscow, *Management*, 1984, ch. 13

867 Imagination continually frustrates tradition; that is its function.
— John Pfeiffer, *New York Times*, March 29, 1979

Inflation

868 Inflation might be called prosperity with high blood pressure.
— Arnold H. Glasow, *Reader's Digest*, Sept., 1966

869 Inflation is like sin; every government denounces it and every government practices it.
— Frederick Leith-Ross, *The Observer*, June 30, 1957

870 Big business is not dangerous because it is big, but because its bigness is an unwholesome inflation created by privileges and exemptions which it ought not to enjoy.

—Woodrow Wilson,
nomination acceptance
speech, July 7, 1912

871 What this country needs is a good five-cent nickel.

—Franklin P. Adams,
Liberty,
Jan. 2, 1943

872 Inflation is as violent as a mugger, as frightening as an armed robber and as deadly as a hit man.

—Ronald Reagan,
Los Angeles Times,
Oct. 20, 1978

873 Steel prices cause inflation like wet sidewalks cause rain.

—Roger Blough,
Forbes,
Aug. 1, 1967

874 When future historians look back on our way of curing inflation ... they'll probably compare it to bloodletting in the Middle Ages.

—Lee Iacocca,
Fortune,
June 27, 1983

Information

875 Intuition becomes increasingly valuable in the new information society precisely because there is so much data.

—John Naisbitt and
Patricia Aburdene,
*Re-inventing the
Corporation,* 1985, ch. 2

876 Everybody gets so much information all day long that they lose their common sense.

—Gertrude Stein,
quoted in *Chicago Tribune,*
June 25, 1978

877 I was brought up to believe that the only thing worth doing was to add to the sum of accurate information in the world.

—Margaret Mead,
New York Times,
Aug. 9, 1964

878 The new source of power is not money in the hands of a few but information in the hands of many.

—John Naisbitt,
Megatrends,
1984, ch. 1

879 The interview that results in no unfavorable information is inescapably a poor interview.

—Richard A. Fear,
The Evaluation Interview,
1973, ch. 2

880 Information is the equalizer; it breaks down the hierarchy. A lot of institutions

are living in a world that is
rapidly passing them by.
— Edmund G. Brown, Jr.,
Esquire, Feb., 1978

881 Not all chief executives
are temperamentally capable of
accepting and assimilating information which happens to
conflict with their personal
values and predilections.
— Robert N. McMurry,
Harvard Business Review,
1965

882 We're drowning in in-
formation and starving for
knowledge.
— Rutherford D. Rogers,
New York Times,
Feb. 25, 1985

883 It is a very sad thing
that nowadays there is so little
useless information.
— Oscar Wilde,
Saturday Review,
Nov. 17, 1894

Intelligence and Intellect

884 Curiosity is one of the
permanent and certain
characteristics of a vigorous
intellect.
— Samuel Johnson,
The Rambler,
1750–1752, no. 103

885 The greater intellect one
has, the more originality one
finds in men. Ordinary persons
find no differences between
men.
— Blaise Pascal,
Pensées, 1670, no. 7

886 There are three classes
of intellects: one which comprehends by itself; another
which appreciates what others
comprehend; and a third which
neither comprehends by itself
nor by showing of others; the
first is the most excellent, the
second is good, and the third is
useless.
— Niccolò Machiavelli,
The Prince, 1513, ch. 22

887 Intelligence is not all
that important in the exercise of
power and is often, in point of
fact, useless.
— Henry A. Kissinger,
Esquire, June, 1975

888 Brilliance without the
capability to communicate it, is
worth little in any enterprise.
— Thomas Leech, *How to
Prepare, Stage, and Deliver
Winning Presentations,*
1982, ch. 1

889 The sublime and the
ridiculous are often so nearly
related, that it is difficult to
class them separately. One step
above the sublime, makes the
ridiculous; and one step above

the ridiculous, makes the
sublime again.
>—Thomas Paine, *The Age of*
>*Reason,* 1795, part II

890 Anti-intellectualism has
long been the anti–Semitism of
the businessman.
>—Arthur M. Schlesinger, Jr.,
>*Partisan Review,*
>March 4, 1953

891 The greatest intellectual
capacities are only found in
connection with a vehement and
passionate will.
>—Arthur Schopenhauer,
>*The World as Will and Idea,*
>1819, book IV

892 In the practical use of
our intellect, forgetting is as important as remembering.
>—William James,
>*The Principles of Psychology,*
>1890, ch. 16

893 It is impossible to
underrate human intelligence—
beginning with one's own.
>—Henry Brooks Adams,
>*Kansas City Star,*
>April 6, 1977

Judgment

894 Judgment comes from
experience, and great judgment
comes from bad experience.
>—Bob Packwood,
>*New York Times,*
>May 30, 1986

895 How dreadful it is when
the right judge judges wrong.
>—Sophocles,
>*Antigone,*
>ca. 440 B.C., line 323

896 Become aware of the
silent conversations you hold
with yourself. Even if you don't
consciously realize it, you are
constantly judging and prejudg-
ing your every action.
>—Denis Waitley and
>Remi L. Witt, *The Joy of*
>*Working,* 1985,
>"Day 2, Self-Talk"

897 It is a sin to believe evil
of others, but it is seldom a
mistake.
>—H.L. Mencken, quoted
>by Robert W. Kent, *Money*
>*Talks,* 1985, "Managers"

898 No one ever became extremely wicked suddenly.
>—Juvenal, *Satires,*
>ca. 110, no. 2

899 Men never do evil so
completely and cheerfully as
when they do it from religious
conviction.
>—Blaise Pascal,
>*Pensées,* 1670, no. 895

900 Men of ill judgment oft
ignore the good that lies within
their hands, till they have lost
it.
>—Sophocles, *Ajax,*
>ca. 445 B.C., line 964

901 I have noted that persons with bad judgment are more insistent that we do what they think best.
— Lionel Abel,
New York Times,
Feb. 6, 1987

902 Experience never errs; what alone may err is our judgment, which predicts effects that cannot be produced by our experiments.
— Leonardo da Vinci,
Notebooks,
ca. 1500, II

903 He hath a good judgment that relieth not wholly on his own.
— Thomas Fuller,
Gnomologia,
1732, no. 1882

904 The judge should not be young; he should have learned to know evil, not from his own soul, but from late and long observation of the nature of evil in others: knowledge should be his guide, not personal experience.
— Plato, *The Republic,*
ca. 370 B.C., book III,
section 409

905 You shall judge of a man by his foes as well as by his friends.
— Joseph Conrad, quoted
by Robert W. Kent, *Money Talks,* 1985, "Managers"

906 The number of those who undergo the fatigue of judging for themselves is very small indeed.
— Richard Brinsley Sheridan,
The Critic, 1779,
act I, scene ii

907 Some circumstantial evidence is very strong, as when you find a trout in the milk.
— Henry David Thoreau,
Journal, Nov., 1850

Justice

908 Justice is truth in action.
— Benjamin Disraeli,
speech, Feb. 11, 1851

909 Forgetting of a wrong is a mild revenge.
— Thomas Fuller,
Gnomologia, 1732, no. 1592

910 The robbed that smiles steals something from the thief.
— William Shakespeare,
Othello, 1605,
act I, scene iii, line 208

911 Living well is the best revenge.
— George Herbert,
Jacula Prudentum,
1651, no. 520

912 Mankind censure justice, fearing that they may be the victims of it and not

because they shrink from committing it.
— Plato, *The Republic,*
ca. 370 B.C., book I,
section 344

913 There is no such thing as justice—in or out of court.
— Clarence Darrow,
New York Times,
April 19, 1936

914 The strictest justice is sometimes the greatest injustice.
— Terence,
Heauton Timorumenos,
163 B.C., line 796

915 A false balance is abomination to the Lord; But a just weight is his delight.
— Bible, Proverbs 11:1

916 Innocence has nothing to dread.
— Jean Racine, *Phèdre,*
1677, act III, scene vi

917 Americans are so enamored of equality that they would rather be equal in slavery than unequal in freedom.
— Alexis de Tocqueville,
Democracy in America, 1835,
volume II, part II, ch. 1

918 The greatest griefs are those we cause ourselves.
— Sophocles, *Oedipus Rex,*
ca. 430 B.C., line 1230

919 Reputation is an idle and most false imposition; oft

got without merit, and lost without deserving.
— William Shakespeare,
Othello, 1605, act II,
scene iii, line 270

920 Reason commands us far more imperiously than a master: when we disobey the latter we are punished; in disobeying the former we are fools.
— Blaise Pascal,
Pensées, 1670, no. 768

921 Society often forgives the criminal, it never forgives the dreamer.
— Oscar Wilde,
Oscariana, 1911

922 Truth is the summit of being; justice is the application of it to affairs.
— Ralph Waldo Emerson,
Essays: Second Series,
1844, "Character"

923 Anybody who gets away with something will come back to get away with a little bit more.
— Harold Schonberg,
New York Times,
Oct. 8, 1972

924 When there is an income tax, the just man will pay more and the unjust man less on the same amount of income.
— Plato, *The Republic,*
ca. 360 B.C.,
book I, section 343

925 Even doubtful accusations leave a stain behind them.
— Thomas Fuller,
Gnomologia,
1732, no. 1395

926 Capitalism without bankruptcy is like Christianity without hell.
— Frank Borman, *US,*
April 21, 1986

927 Evil deeds do not prosper; the slow man catches up with the swift.
— Homer, *The Odyssey,*
ca. 550 B.C.,
book VIII, line 329

928 The public seldom forgives twice.
— Johann Kaspar Lavater,
Aphorisms on Man,
1788, no. 606

929 Everyone is bound to bear patiently the results of his own example.
— Phaedrus, *Fables,*
ca. 10 B.C., book I,
fable 26, line 12

930 You're never too bad to win.
— Tom McElligott,
Wall Street Journal,
March 26, 1987

931 Injustice is relatively easy to bear; what stings is justice.
— H.L. Mencken, *Prejudices,*
Third Series, 1922, ch. 3

Knowledge

932 Knowledge is the antidote to fear.
— Ralph Waldo Emerson,
Society and Solitude, 1870,
volume III, "Courage"

933 Emancipation from error is the condition of real knowledge.
— Henri Frédéric Amiel,
Amiel's Journal 1849–1872,
Aug. 30, 1872

934 He that knows least commonly presumes most.
— Thomas Fuller,
Gnomologia,
1732, no. 2208

935 People who hire the most often know the least about hiring.
— Robert Half,
Robert Half on Hiring,
1985, introduction

936 'Tis not knowing much, but what is useful, that makes a man wise.
— Thomas Fuller,
Gnomologia,
1732, no. 5097

937 In the industrial age, when the strategic resource was capital, the goal of the corporation could only have been profits. In the information era, however, the strategic resource

is information, knowledge, creativity.
— John Naisbitt and Patricia Aburdene, *Re-inventing the Corporation,* 1985, ch. 1

938 It is possible to fly without motors, but not without knowledge and skill.
— Wilbur Wright, letter, 1900

939 People don't care how much you know, until they know how much you care . . . about them.
— Zig Ziglar, *Top Performance,* 1982, ch. 6

940 Knowledge fills a large brain; it merely inflates a small one.
— Sydney J. Harris, *Detroit Free Press,* Jan. 7, 1982

941 All men by nature desire to know.
— Aristotle, *Metaphysics,* ca. 330 B.C., book I, ch. 1

942 To be able to know is the same as to know.
— The Universal Self-Instructor, 1883, "Legal Maxims"

943 Greatness knows itself.
— William Shakespeare, *Henry IV, Part I,* 1598, act IV, scene iii, line 74

944 Get to know what it is you don't know as fast as you can.
— Robert Heller, *The Super Managers,* 1984, ch. 10

945 The desire of knowledge, like the thirst of riches, increases ever with the acquisition of it.
— Laurence Sterne, *Tristram Shandy,* 1760, book II, ch. 3

946 Knowledge is proud that he has learned so much; Wisdom is humble that he knows no more.
— William Cowper, *The Task,* 1785, part IV, "Winter Walk at Noon," line 96

947 I have tried to know absolutely nothing about a great many things, and I have succeeded fairly well.
— Robert Benchley, *Rocky Mountain News,* April 23, 1980

948 Order and simplification are the first steps toward the mastery of a subject — the actual enemy is the unknown.
— Thomas Mann, *The Magic Mountain,* 1924, ch. 5

949 Never acquire a business you don't know how to run.
— Robert W. Johnson,
Dun's Review,
Dec., 1970

950 Integrity without knowledge is weak and useless, and knowledge without integrity is dangerous and dreadful.
— Samuel Johnson,
Rasselas, 1759, ch. XI

951 The most useful instinct is trained instinct.
— Henry O. Golightly,
Managing with Style,
1977, ch. 2

952 He that hath knowledge spareth his words; and a man of understanding is of an excellent spirit.
— Bible, Proverbs 17:27

953 Our knowledge is a little island in a great ocean of nonknowledge.
— Isaac Bashevis Singer,
New York Times,
Dec. 3, 1978

954 I'm astounded by people who want to "know" the universe when it's hard enough to find your way around China-town.
— Woody Allen, quoted by
Robert Byrne, *The 637 Best Things Anybody Ever Said,*
1982, no. 22

Law and Lawyers

955 *Lawsuit, n.* a machine which you go into as a pig and come out as a sausage.
— Ambrose Bierce,
The Devil's Dictionary, 1906

956 Law is a flag and gold is the wind that makes it wave.
— Russian proverb

957 We must not make a scarecrow of the law,
Setting it up to fear the birds of prey,
And let it keep one shape, till custom make it
Their perch, and not their terror.
— William Shakespeare,
Measure for Measure, 1605,
act II, scene i, line 1

958 There is no man so good who, were he to submit his thoughts to the laws, would not deserve hanging ten times in his life.
— Michel Eyquem
de Montaigne, *Essays,*
1580–1595,
book III, ch. 1

959 The first thing we do, let's kill all the lawyers.
— William Shakespeare,
Henry VI, Part II, 1591,
act IV, scene ii, line 86

960 Why may not that be the skull of a lawyer? Where be his quiddities now, his quillets,

his cases and his tenures, and his tricks?
— William Shakespeare, *Hamlet,* 1601, act V, scene i, line 104

961 We were not born to sue, but to command.
— William Shakespeare, *Richard II,* 1595, act I, scene i, line 196

962 I have always noticed that any time a man can't come and settle with you without bringing his lawyer, why, look out for him.
— Will Rogers, quoted by Richard M. Ketchum, *Will Rogers, His Life and Times,* 1973, page 188

Leadership

963 Authority, and how it is used, tells the story of most organizations.
— Woodrow H. Sears, Jr., *Back in Working Order,* 1984, ch. 3

964 The graveyards are full of indispensable men.
— Charles de Gaulle (attributed)

965 Leadership, like life, can only be learned as you go along.
— Harold Geneen with Alvin Moscow, *Managing,* 1984, ch. 6

966 While business certainly needs managers to make the trains run on time, it more desperately needs heroes to get the engine going.
— Terrence E. Deal and Allen A. Kennedy, *Corporate Cultures,* 1982, ch. 3

967 Leadership is the very heart and soul of business management. No one really manages a business by shuffling the numbers or rearranging organizational charts or applying the latest business school formulas. What you manage in business is people.
— Harold Geneen with Alvin Moscow, *Managing,* 1984, ch. 6

968 Despite all you hear about participative management, the chief executive still casts a long shadow.
— Joel E. Ross and Michael J. Kami, *Corporate Management in Crisis: Why the Mighty Fall,* 1973, ch. 19

969 We have yet to find a significant case where the company did not move in the direction of the chief executive's home.
— Ken Patton, *New York Times,* Feb. 5, 1971

970 What short-term CEO will take a long-run view when

it lowers his own income? Only a saint, and there aren't very many saints.

— Lester C. Thurow,
Newsweek, Dec. 7, 1981

971 The person who knows "how" will always have a job. The person who knows "why" will always be his boss.

— Diane Ravitch, *Time,*
June 17, 1985

972 Avoid one-man rule. The autocratic leader — however capable — can't be stretched far enough to run today's complex company. Besides, who will replace him?

— Joel E. Ross and Michael
J. Kami, *Corporate
Management in Crisis: Why
the Mighty Fall,* 1973, ch. 8

973 The executive task is essentially custodial. Once the huge empire has been created, it must be protected and preserved by the curator-executive.

— Deaver Brown,
The Entrepreneur's Guide,
1980, ch. 1

974 A manager multiplies his own knowledge and skills when he imparts them to his subordinates. When he can transfer the knowledge and skills of other capable people to his employees, he increases

their value by another order of magnitude.

— Lester R. Bittel,
*The Nine Master Keys of
Management,* 1972, ch. 8

975 The true leader is always led.

Carl G. Jung, *Guardian
Weekly,* Oct. 30, 1976

976 I start with the premise that the function of leadership is to produce more leaders, not more followers.

— Ralph Nader,
Time, Nov. 8, 1976

977 In an organization, doing is causing people to have a productivity that makes everything happen on time and profitably. The attitude of doing comes from the leader's attitude.

— Philip B. Crosby,
Running Things, 1986, ch. 7

978 The inherent preferences of organizations are clarity, certainty, and perfection. The inherent nature of human relationships involves ambiguity, uncertainty, and imperfection. How one honors, balances, and integrates the needs of both is the real trick of management.

— Richard Tanner Pascale
and Anthony G. Athos,
*The Art of Japanese
Management,* 1981

979 A perfect example of Management by Example and inspirational leadership, Joan of Arc, was rewarded for her heroism by being burned at the stake. Martyrdom is a logical but seemingly inappropriate extension of Management by Example in the military, and probably in business as well.
— Nicholas V. Iuppa, *Management by Guilt,* 1985, part 2

980 Lesson for stockholders and directors: If the chief executive doesn't retire gracefully after five or six years — throw the rascal out.
— Robert Townsend, *Further Up the Organization,* 1984, "Wearing Out Your Welcome"

981 Don't be afraid of youth. Capability as a manager is not a function of age or experience. Get some tigers in the company.
— Joel E. Ross and Michael J. Kami, *Corporate Management in Crisis: Why the Mighty Fall,* 1973, ch. 8

982 For all the intellect and technique a manager can muster, his success turns on a subtle, elusive quality — the degree to which he can stimulate people to make the most of their own inherent capabilities.
— Lester R. Bittel, *The Nine Master Keys of Management,* 1972, overview

983 What the work force really wants is management leadership whose competence and concern they can trust.
— Zig Ziglar, *Top Performance,* 1982, ch. 12

984 We aren't producing leaders like we used to. A new chief executive officer today, exhausted by the climb to the peak, falls down on the mountaintop and goes to sleep.
— Robert Townsend, *Further Up the Organization,* 1984, "Leadership"

985 Leaders often just do not realize what they can cause if they permit the impression to exist that there is room for dishonesty in any form in their world. Fuses are lit all over the place. Who knows where they will lead?
— Philip B. Crosby, *Running Things,* 1986, ch. 5

986 Beware the company with a sacred cow at its helm. Sacred cows rarely make anything happen; they want things to work as they've always worked and thus can be blindsided in a crisis.
— Terrence E. Deal and Allen A. Kennedy, *Corporate Cultures,* 1982, ch. 3

987 It is not well that there should be many masters; one man must be supreme.
— Homer, *The Iliad,*
ca. 550 B.C.,
book II, line 204

988 If we take the term in the strict sense, there never has been a real democracy, and there never will be. It is against the natural order for the many to govern and the few to be governed.
— Jean-Jacques Rousseau,
The Social Contract,
1762, book III, ch. 4

989 Accountants can be smarter than anybody else or more ambitious or both, but essentially they are bean counters — their job is to serve the operations. They can't run the ship.
— Robert Townsend, *Further Up the Organization,* 1984,
"Accounting and Reporting"

990 Anyone can hold the helm when the sea is calm.
— Publilius Syrus,
Maxims, 1st
century B.C., no. 358

Learning

991 Learning is discovering that something is possible.
— Fritz Perls,
Omni, Nov., 1979

992 Diligence is a great teacher.
— Arabic proverb

993 The trouble with most men of learning is that their learning goes to their heads.
— Isaac Goldberg,
Reflex, Dec., 1927

994 He listens well who takes note.
— Dante, *The Divine Comedy,*
ca. 1315, "Inferno,"
canto XV, line 99

995 He who learns but does not think, is lost. He who thinks but does not learn is in great danger.
— Confucius, *Analects,*
ca. 500 B.C.,
book II, ch. 5

996 Tradition does not mean that the living are dead, it means that the dead are living.
— Harold Macmillan,
Manchester Guardian,
Dec. 18, 1958

997 That men do not learn very much from the lessons of history is the most important of all the lessons of history.
— Aldous Huxley,
Collected Essays, 1959

998 It would be ironic if significant new insights about how we learn would come, not

from the academy, but from industry and business.
> —Ernest Boyer,
> *New York Times,*
> Jan. 28, 1985

999 Every young man should have a hobby. Learning how to handle money is the best one.
> —Jack Hurley, quoted
> by Robert W. Kent,
> *Money Talks,* 1985,
> "Microeconomics"

1000 To teach is to learn twice.
> —Joseph Joubert,
> *Pensées,* 1842

Leisure

1001 *Clinomania, n.* excessive desire to stay in bed.
> —Josefa Heifetz Byrne,
> *Mrs. Byrne's Dictionary,* 1974

1002 The time to relax is when you don't have time for it.
> —Sydney J. Harris, quoted
> by Peter Potter, *All About*
> *Success,* 1988, "Relaxation"

1003 If all the year were playing holidays,
To sport would be as tedious as to work.
> —William Shakespeare,
> *Henry IV, Part I,* 1598,
> act I, scene ii, line 227

1004 A life spent in constant labor is a life wasted, save a man be such a fool as to regard a fulsome obituary notice as an ample reward.
> —George Jean Nathan,
> *Living Philosophies,* 1931

1005 Bowmen bend their bows when they wish to shoot; unbrace them when the shooting is over. Were they kept always strung they would break and fail the archer in time of need. So it is with men. If they give themselves constantly to serious work, and never indulge awhile in pastime or sport, they lose their senses and become mad.
> —Herodotus,
> *The History,*
> ca. 450 B.C.,
> book II, ch. 173

1006 We continue to overlook the fact that work has become a leisure activity.
> —Mark Abrams,
> *The Observer,*
> June 3, 1962

1007 It is sweet to let the mind unbend on occasion.
> —Horace, *Epodes IV,*
> 13 B.C., stanza XII, line 27

1008 The busiest men have the most leisure.
> —English proverb

Lending

1009 When it's your money, you tend to spend it more wisely.
— George Hernandez, *Hispanic Business,* June, 1987

1010 A financier is a pawnbroker with imagination.
— Arthur Wing Pinero, quoted by Robert W. Kent, *Money Talks,* 1985, "Finance"

1011 It's better to give than to lend, and it costs about the same.
— Philip Gibbs, quoted by Robert W. Kent, *Money Talks,* 1985, "Finance"

1012 Neither a borrower, nor a lender be;
For loan oft loses both itself and friend,
And borrowing dulls the edge of husbandry.
This above all: to thine own self be true,
And it must follow, as the night the day,
Thou canst not then be false to any man.
— William Shakespeare, *Hamlet,* 1601, act I, scene iii, line 75

1013 Nowhere is a man's imagination so fertile as in the discovery of new ways to say no to a man who asks for money.
— Joseph H. Shapiro, *Chicago,* Sept., 1977

1014 The rich ruleth over the poor, and the borrower is servant to the lender.
— Bible, Proverbs 22:7

1015 I don't know of anything so remorseless on the face of the earth than seven percent interest.
— Henry Wheeler Shaw, quoted by Robert W. Kent, *Money Talks,* 1985, "Finance"

1016 Be not made a beggar by banqueting upon borrowing.
— Bible: Apocrypha, Ecclesiasticus 18:33

1017 Live within your income, even if you have to borrow money to do so.
— Henry Wheeler Shaw, quoted by Robert W. Kent, *Money Talks,* 1985, "Finance"

Lies

1018 Lying is an elementary means of self-defense.
— Susan Sontag, *Saturday Review,* Sept. 23, 1972

1019 Lord, Lord, how this world is given to lying!
—William Shakespeare,
Henry IV, Part I, 1598,
act V, scene iv, line 148

1020 If you begin by saying, "Thou shalt not lie," there is no longer any possibility of political action.
—Jean-Paul Sartre,
Time, April 28, 1980

1021 Lies are essential to humanity. They are perhaps as important as the pursuit of pleasure and moreover are dictated by that pursuit.
—Marcel Proust,
Remembrance of Things Past,
1913–1926, volume VI,
"The Sweet Cheat Gone"

1022 Take the life-lie away from the average man and straight away you take away his happiness.
—Henrik Ibsen,
The Wild Duck,
1984, act V

1023 If there were no falsehoods in the world, there would be no doubt; if there were no doubt, there would be no inquiry; if no inquiry, no wisdom, no knowledge; no genius.
—Walter Savage Landor,
Imaginary Conversations,
1824–1829

1024 Nostalgia is a seductive liar.
—George Ball,
Newsweek,
March 22, 1971

1025 A liar should have a good memory.
—Quintilian,
Institutio Oratoria,
1st century A.D., book 4

1026 Anyone who does not feel sufficiently strong in memory should not meddle with lying.
—Michel Eyquem de
Montaigne, *Essays,*
1580–1595,
book I, ch. 9

1027 In the war between falsehood and truth, falsehood wins the first battle and truth the last.
—Mujibur Rahman,
Newsweek, Jan. 24, 1972

1028 The cruelest lies are often told in silence.
—Robert Louis Stevenson,
Virginibus Puerisque,
1881, I, ch. 4,
"The Truth of Intercourse"

1029 The most common lie is that with which one lies to oneself; lying to others is relatively an exception.
—Friedrich Nietzsche,
The Anti-Christ,
1888, aphorism 55

1030 Sometimes we have to change the truth in order to remember it.
— George Santayana, *Time,* July 28, 1975

1031 One of the most striking differences between a cat and a lie is that a cat has only nine lives.
— Mark Twain, *Pudd'nhead Wilson,* 1894, ch. 7

1032 It is hard to believe that a man is telling the truth when you know you would lie in his place.
— H.L. Mencken, quoted by Robert W. Kent, *Money Talks,* 1985, "Managers"

1033 Truth is not only violated by falsehood; it may be outraged by silence.
— Henri Frédéric Amiel, *Amiel's Journal 1849–1872,* Dec. 17, 1856

1034 The income tax has made more liars out of the American people than golf has.
— Will Rogers, quoted by Richard M. Ketchum, *Will Rogers, His Life and Times,* 1973, page 400

Luck

1035 Success is simply a matter of luck. Ask any failure.
— Earl Wilson, quoted by Peter Potter, *All About Success,* 1988, "Luck"

1036 We must believe in luck. For how else can we explain the success of those we don't like?
— Jean Cocteau, quoted by Robert Byrne, *The Other 637 Best Things Anybody Ever Said,* 1984, no. 528

1037 A wise man turns chance into good fortune.
— Thomas Fuller, *Gnomologia,* 1732, no. 475

1038 It cannot be ignored that *Luck* and *Opportunity* often win the race, while *Merit* and *Ability* lag behind, but those who have "greatness thrust upon them" are few and far between.
— The Universal Self-Instructor, 1883, "Business Habits"

1039 I am a great believer in luck, and I find the harder I work the more I have of it.
— Stephen Leacock, quoted by Robert W. Kent, *Money Talks,* 1985, "Entrepreneurs"

1040 Chance favors the trained mind.
— Louis Pasteur, *The Sciences,* 1981

1041 Do not be overly elated by good fortune. Remember how easily it can change.
— Aesop, fable, "Memento Mori," ca. 550 B.C.

1042 Nothing is more humiliating than to see idiots succeed in enterprises we have failed in.
—Gustave Flaubert,
quoted by Robert W. Kent,
Money Talks,
1985, "Managers"

1043 Luck is infatuated with the efficient.
—Persian proverb

1044 Fortune brings in some boats that are not steered.
—William Shakespeare,
Cymbeline, 1610,
act IV, scene iii, line 46

1045 Our banking system grew by accident; and whenever something happens by accident, it becomes a religion.
—Walter Wriston,
Business Week,
Jan. 20, 1975

1046 I feel like a fugitive from th' law of averages.
—Bill Mauldin,
Up Front, 1946

Mediocrity

1047 *Hyperhedonia, n.* abnormal pleasure from doing ho-hum things.
—Josefa Heifetz Byrne,
Mrs. Byrne's Dictionary, 1974

1048 Only a mediocre person is always at his best.
—William Somerset Maugham,
Forbes, Aug. 1, 1977

1049 The business world worships mediocrity. Officially we revere free enterprise, initiative and individuality. Unofficially we fear it.
—George Lois, quoted
by Robert W. Kent,
Money Talks, 1985,
"Business Is and Business As"

1050 Mediocrity requires aloofness to preserve its dignity.
—Charles G. Dawes,
quoted by Peter Potter,
All About Success,
1988, "Mediocrity"

1051 Attention to details is not nitpicking but an essential and vital part of successful management.
—Joel E. Ross and Michael
J. Kami, *Corporate Management in Crisis: Why the
Mighty Fall,* 1973, ch. 7

1052 Great innovators and original thinkers and artists attract the wrath of mediocrities as lightning rods draw the flashes.
—Theodor Reik,
The Need to Be Loved,
1963, part I, no. 4

1053 Mediocre minds usually dismiss anything which

reaches beyond their own understanding.

> —François, Duc de la Rochefoucauld, *Reflections; or, Sentences and Moral Maxims,* 1665, maxim 375

1054 If you are mediocre and you grovel, you shall succeed.

> —Pierre de Beaumarchais, *The Marriage of Figaro,* 1784, act III, scene iii

1055 Excessive standardization destroys flexibility, dampers creativity and creates uniform mediocrity.

> —Joel E. Ross and Michael J. Kami, *Corporate Management in Crisis: Why the Mighty Fall,* 1973, ch. 9

1056 Every effort that one produces gives one an enemy. To be popular one must be a mediocrity.

> —Oscar Wilde, *Oscariana,* 1911

1057 Don't rationalize mediocrity.

> —George W. Miller, *Time,* July 17, 1978

Meetings

1058 *Anthropophobia, n.* fear of meeting people; fear of society.

> —Josefa Heifetz Byrne, *Mrs. Byrne's Dictionary,* 1974

1059 There is no crisis to which academics will not respond with a seminar.

> —Anonymous

1060 A conference is a gathering of important people who, singly, can do nothing but together can decide that nothing can be done.

> —Fred Allen, letter, Jan. 25, 1940

1061 There is no better place in the world to find out the shortcomings of each other than a conference.

> —Will Rogers, quoted by Richard M. Ketchum, *Will Rogers, His Life and Times,* 1973, page 189

1062 Never dump a good idea on a conference table. It will belong to the conference.

> —Jane Trahey, *New York Times,* Sept. 18, 1977

1063 A committee is a thing which takes a week to do what one good man can do in an hour.

> —Elbert Hubbard, quoted by Peter Potter, *All About Success,* 1988, "Cooperation"

1064 Outside of traffic, there is nothing that has held this

country back as much as committees.
> — Will Rogers, quoted by
> Richard M. Ketchum,
> *Will Rogers, His Life
> and Times,* 1973, page 281

1065 In a small company, one person's hunch can be enough to launch a new product. In a big company, the same concept is likely to be buried in committees for months.
> — Al Ries and Jack Trout,
> *Marketing Warfare,*
> 1986, ch. 10

1066 The less you enjoy serving on committees, the more likely you are to be pressured to do so.
> — Charles Issawi,
> *The Columbia Forum,*
> Summer, 1970

1067 In a good meeting there is a momentum that comes from the spontaneous exchange of fresh ideas and produces extraordinary results. That momentum depends on the freedom permitted the participants.
> — Harold Geneen,
> *Fortune,* Oct. 15, 1984

1068 Don't try to manage from any board of directors — or any other kind of meeting.
> — Robert Heller,
> *The Super Managers,*
> 1984, ch. 9

1069 The length of a meeting rises with the square of the number of people present.
> — Robert K. Mueller, *Board
> Life,* 1974, ch. 11

1070 The usefulness of a meeting is in inverse proportion to the attendance.
> — Lane Kirkland,
> *Wall Street Journal,*
> March 3, 1974

1071 Round tables help create good peer relations among meeting participants; tables with distinct heads reinforce hierarchies.
> — Terrence E. Deal and
> Allen A. Kennedy,
> *Corporate Cultures,*
> 1982, ch. 4

1072 While few managers would own up to it, most "participation" is honorific and empty. It is a standing joke that when you become too senior to work, then your work is going to meetings.
> — Woodrow H. Sears, Jr.,
> *Back in Working Order,*
> 1984, ch. 3

1073 The real process of making decisions, of gathering support, of developing opinions, happens before the meeting — or after.
> — Terrence E. Deal and
> Allen A. Kennedy,
> *Corporate Cultures,* 1982, ch. 5

1074 Try skipping a meeting if you want to find out how important it is.
— Robert Townsend,
Further Up the Organization,
1984, "Feedback:
Tell Them Everything"

1075 Those who are absent are always wrong.
— English proverb

Memos

1076 I'm just not a memo writer. I like to look someone in the eye and say, "Let's talk."
— Peter L. Scott,
Sky Magazine, Aug. 1, 1987

1077 "The horror of that moment," the King went on, "I shall never, *never* forget!"
"You will, though," the Queen said, "if you don't make a memorandum of it."
— Lewis Carroll,
*Through the Looking-
Glass,* 1872, ch. 1

1078 I have received memos so swollen with managerial babble that they struck me as the literary equivalent of assault with a deadly weapon.
— Peter Baida,
American Heritage, April, 1985

1079 The only way to find out if a memo or a report is

unnecessary is to read the darn thing — which could turn out to be a waste of time.
— *Supervisor's Bulletin,*
Oct. 30, 1985, no. 744

1080 I for one appreciate a good form letter, having worked on Capitol Hill and learned seven dozen cordial ways to say nothing.
— Carrie Johnson,
New York Times,
July 14, 1984

1081 A memorandum is written not to inform the reader but to protect the writer.
— Dean Acheson,
Wall Street Journal,
Sept. 18, 1977

1082 Here are a few of the unpleasant'st words
That ever blotted paper.
— William Shakespeare,
The Merchant of Venice, 1596,
act III, scene ii, line 252

1083 Notes are often necessary, but they are necessary evils.
— Samuel Johnson,
*Plays of William
Shakespeare, with Notes,*
1765, preface

1084 Let there be gall enough in thy ink.
— William Shakespeare,
Twelfth Night, 1600,
act III, scene ii, line 54

1085 All right, as long as I get the memo.
—A.J. Carothers,
*The Secret of My
Success,* 1987

Misfortune

1086 *Deflagrable, adj.* pertaining to a sudden bursting into flame, sudden vaporization, or fast burning.
—Josefa Heifetz Byrne,
Mrs. Byrne's Dictionary, 1974

1087 Anything that happens enough times to irritate you will happen at least once more.
—Tom Parkins,
Omni, May, 1979

1088 For as fortunes sharp advertisee
The worst kinde of infortunate is this,
A man to have ben in prosperitee,
And 'it remembren, when it passed is.
—Geoffrey Chaucer,
Troilus and Cressida,
ca. 1380, book III,
stanza 233

1089 We all have strength enough to endure the misfortune of others.
—François, Duc de la Rochefoucauld, *Reflections;
or, Sentences and Moral
Maxims,* 1665, maxim 19

1090 Never find your delight in another's misfortune.
—Publilius Syrus,
Maxims, 1st century,
B.C., no. 467

1091 Everything is funny as long as it is happening to somebody else.
—Will Rogers,
Kansas City Star,
April 10, 1977

1092 In the days of prosperity there is a forgetfulness of affliction: and in the day of affliction there is no more remembrance of prosperity.
—Bible: Apocrypha,
Ecclesiasticus 11:25

1093 Driving 'round a bend and skidding on a mat of dead toads is very unpleasant for all concerned.
—Amanda Hillier,
New York Times,
March 14, 1987

Money

1094 *Make ends meet, v. phr.* to have enough money to pay one's bills; earn what it costs to live.
—Maxine Tull Boatner,
J. Edward Gates, and
Adam Makkai, *A Dictionary
of American Idioms,* 1987

1095 Money is just something to make bookkeeping convenient.

> —H.L. Hunt,
> *Time,* Dec. 9, 1974

1096 When money is not a servant it is a master.

> —Italian proverb

1097 Money is a new form of slavery, and distinguished from the old simply by the fact that it is impersonal, that there is no human relation between master and slave.

> —Leo Tolstoy, *What Are We To Do?*, 1891

1098 Money alone sets all the world in motion.

> —Publilius Syrus,
> *Maxims,* 1st century
> B.C., no. 656

1099 Money speaks sense in a language all nations understand.

> —Aphra Behn,
> *The Rover, Part II,*
> 1680, act III, scene i

1100 Money never cometh out of season.

> —Thomas Draxe,
> *Bibliotheca scholastica*
> *instructissima,* 1616

1101 When the foundation of a pyramid erodes, the top can still be supported on nothing but money.

> —Laurence J. Peter,
> *Why Things Go Wrong,*
> 1985, ch. 5

1102 Nothing so evil as money ever grew to be current among men.

> —Sophocles,
> *Antigone,*
> ca. 440 B.C., line 295

1103 Young people, nowadays, imagine that money is everything, and when they grow older they know it.

> —Oscar Wilde,
> *New West,* Feb., 1977

1104 Money is always on the brain as long as there is a brain in reasonable order.

> —Samuel Butler,
> *Notebooks,* 1912

1105 The universal regard for money is the one hopeful fact in our civilization.

> —George Bernard Shaw,
> *Major Barbara,*
> 1905, preface

1106 Money is flat and meant to be piled up.

> —Scottish proverb

1107 If you can count your money, you don't have a billion dollars.

> —J. Paul Getty, *International Herald Tribune,* Jan. 10, 1961

1108 The value of money is that with it you can tell anyone to go to the devil.
— William Somerset Maugham (attributed)

1109 A man without money is like a wolf without teeth.
— French proverb

1110 Money is like a sixth sense without which you cannot make a complete use of the other five.
— William Somerset Maugham, *Of Human Bondage*, 1915, ch. 51

1111 One bag of money is stronger than two bags of truth.
— Danish proverb

1112 With money one may command devils; without it, one cannot even summon a man.
— Chinese proverb

1113 It is not the volume of money but the activity of money that counts.
— W. Bourke Cockran, speech, Aug. 18, 1896

1114 When a man says money can do anything, that settles it: he hasn't any.
— Edgar Watson Howe, quoted by Robert W. Kent, *Money Talks*, 1985, "Control"

1115 O money, money, how blindly thou hast been wor-shipped, and how stupidly abused!
— Charles Lamb, letter, June 7, 1809

1116 But what certainty is there about money, which, after all, holds all the world together? It depends on the good will of a few capitalists to keep to the agreement that one metal is worth more than another.
— Ivar Kreuger, *New Yorker* Magazine, Oct. 13, 1959

1117 Can anybody remember when the times were not hard and money not scarce?
— Ralph Waldo Emerson, *Work and Days*, 1870

1118 Money is always there but the pockets change.
— Gertrude Stein, *Time,* Oct. 13, 1975

1119 A full pocketbook often groans more loudly than an empty stomach.
— Franklin D. Roosevelt, speech, Nov. 1, 1940

1120 If you have no money, be polite.
— Danish proverb

Motivation

1121 *Goadsman, n.* a man who uses a *goad,* or pointed

stick, to urge his plow horses onward.
— Josefa Heifetz Byrne, *Mrs. Byrne's Dictionary,* 1974

1122 The uncommitted life isn't worth living.
— Marshall W. Fishwick, *Saturday Review,* Dec. 21, 1963

1123 Management must manage! It is a very simple credo, probably the closest thing to the secret of success in business. The strange thing is that everybody knows it, but somehow managers forget it all the time.
— Harold Geneen, *Fortune,* Oct. 1, 1984

1124 Good managers know what they must do and how to go about doing it. They know how to get people of ordinary ability to perform in an extraordinary manner.
— Ronald Brown, *The Practical Manager's Guide to Excellence in Management,* 1979, ch. 2

1125 The conventional definition of management is getting work done through people, but real management is developing people through work.
— Agha Hasan Abedi, *Leaders,* July, 1984

1126 Pay as much attention to your inside image as you do to your outside one. What your employees think of the company — your attitudinal strategy — is an essential motivational device.
— Joel E. Ross and Michael J. Kami, *Corporate Management in Crisis: Why the Mighty Fall,* 1973, ch. 19

1127 The labor of a human being is not a commodity or article of commerce. You can't weigh the soul of a man with a bar of pig-iron.
— Samuel Gompers, *Seventy Years of Life and Labor,* 1925, volume II, ch. 36

1128 People just starting their careers may think a job is just a job. But when they choose a company, they often choose a way of life.
— Terrence E. Deal and Allen A. Kennedy, *Corporate Cultures,* 1982, ch. 1

1129 When you identify with your company's purpose, when you experience ownership in a shared vision, you find yourself doing your life's work instead of just doing time.
— John Naisbitt and Patricia Aburdene, *Re-inventing the Corporation,* 1985, ch. 1

1130 It is always with the best intentions that the worst work is done.
— Oscar Wilde,
Intentions, 1891

1131 I have never known much good done by those who affected to trade for the public good.
— Adam Smith, *Wealth of Nations,* 1776, volume I, book IV, ch. 2

1132 The public may be willing to forgive us for mistakes in judgment but it will not forgive us for mistakes in motive.
— Robert W. Haack,
Wall Street Journal,
Oct. 17, 1967

1133 A hidden intention is a bad one.
— The Universal Self-Instructor, 1883,
"Legal Maxims"

1134 We would often be ashamed of our noblest actions if all their motives were known.
— François, Duc de la Rochefoucauld, *Reflections; or, Sentences and Moral Maxims,* 1665, maxim 409

1135 No mortal man has ever served at the same time his passions and his best interests.
— Sallust, *The War with Catiline,* ca. 40 B.C., ch. LI

1136 Is life worth living? It is, if you take the risk of getting up in the morning and going through the day's work.
— Walter Persegati,
New York Times,
July 9, 1984

1137 The heart has its reasons which reason does not understand.
— Blaise Pascal,
Pensées, 1670, no. 423

Necessity

1138 Necessity is the law of time and place.
— The Universal Self-Instructor, 1883,
"Legal Maxims"

1139 That which is necessary is never a risk.
— Paul de Gondi,
Memoirs,
1665, book II

1140 The word 'necessary' seldom is.
— Keith W. Hall,
Washingtonian,
Nov., 1979

1141 The man who wrestles with necessity, I esteem a fool.
— Euripides,
Mad Heracles,
ca. 410 B.C., line 281

1142 I go on working for the same reason that a hen goes on laying eggs.
— H.L. Mencken, quoted by Robert W. Kent, *Money Talks,* 1985, "Business Is and Business As"

1143 Necessity never made a good bargain.
— Benjamin Franklin, *Poor Richard's Almanac,* April, 1735

Observation

1144 *Autoptic, adj.* pertaining to evidence based on observation.
— Josefa Heifetz Byrne, *Mrs. Byrne's Dictionary,* 1974

1145 The true science and study of man is man.
— Pierre Charron, *De la Sagesse,* 1601, book I, ch. 1

1146 The law of unintended consequences pushes us ceaselessly through the years, permitting no pause for perspective.
— Richard Schickel, *Time,* Nov. 28, 1983

1147 Observe the opportunity.
— Bible: Apocrypha, Ecclesiasticus 4:20

1148 Where observation is concerned, chance favors only the prepared mind.
— Louis Pasteur, address, Dec. 7, 1854

1149 You can observe a lot just by watching.
— Yogi Berra, *Omni,* May, 1979

1150 How much trouble he avoids who does not look to see what his neighbor says or does or thinks.
— Marcus Aurelius Antoninus, *Meditations,* 2nd century A.D., book IV, no. 18

1151 As I grow older, I pay less attention to what men say. I just watch what they do.
— Andrew Carnegie, quoted by Peter Potter, *All About Success,* 1988, "Action"

Office Politics

1152 You lose a lot of time hating people.
— Marian Anderson, *New York Times,* April 18, 1965

1153 Politics is the process of getting along with the querulous, the garrulous and the congenitally unlovable.
— Marilyn Moats Kennedy, *Newsweek,* Sept. 16, 1985

1154 It is well known what a middleman is: he is a man who bamboozles one party and plunders the other.
— Benjamin Disraeli,
speech, April 11, 1845

1155 If self-interest is your goal, you don't understand the problem. You also don't know the law: Give to get.
— Jeffrey G. Allen,
Surviving Corporate Downsizing, 1988, ch. 5

1156 Those who plot against their friends often find to their surprise that they destroy themselves in the bargain.
— Aesop, fable,
"The Fox Out-Foxed,"
ca. 550 B.C.

1157 The president of our company says he's surrounded by yes men. He told me so himself, and I agreed with him.
— Anonymous

1158 Sharks have been swimming the oceans un-challenged for thousands of years; chances are, the species that roams corporate waters will prove just as hardy.
— Eric Gelman,
Newsweek,
Oct. 1, 1984

1159 Don't hire a master to paint you a masterpiece and then assign a roomful of school-boy-artists to look over his shoulder and suggest improvements.
— Robert Townsend,
Further Up the Organization,
1984, "Advertising"

1160 Only the fittest will survive, and the fittest will be the ones who understand their office's politics.
— Jean Hollands,
Newsweek, Sept. 16, 1985

1161 Cabals are everywhere in organizations. Cabals can be large — for example, the membership of the Republican Party. Or a cabal can be as cozy as two people who always second one another's ideas in meetings.
— Terrence E. Deal and
Allen A. Kennedy,
Corporate Cultures,
1982, ch. 5

1162 Everything begins in mysticism and ends in politics.
— Charles Péguy,
Basic Verities: Prose and Poetry, 1943

1163 Frightened people play office politics; they won't come forward, admitting their problems early enough for them to be solved. Capable, independent people leave, not willing to work under those conditions.
— Harold Geneen,
Fortune, Oct. 15, 1984

1164 "Do other men for they would do you." That's the true business precept.
— Charles Dickens,
Martin Chuzzlewit,
1844, ch. 11

1165 Few things are harder to put up with than the annoyance of a good example.
— Mark Twain,
Pudd'nhead Wilson,
1894, ch. 19

Opinions

1166 Common sense is the collection of prejudices acquired by age eighteen.
— Albert Einstein,
Scientific American,
Feb., 1976

1167 There is no right or wrong. There is only opinion.
— A.J. Carothers,
*The Secret of My
Success,* 1987

1168 New opinions are always suspected, and usually opposed, without any other reason but because they are not already common.
— John Locke, *An Essay
Concerning Human Understanding,*
1690, dedicatory epistle

1169 You are young, and the advance of time will make you reverse many of the opinions which you now hold. Wait awhile, and do not attempt to judge at present of the highest things.
— Plato, *Laws,*
ca. 350 B.C.,
Book X, section 888

1170 My advice to any young person at the beginning of their career is to try to look for the mere outlines of big things, with their fresh, untrained, and unprejudiced mind.
— Hans Selye, quoted by
Roger von Oech, *A Kick
in the Seat of the Pants,*
1986, "The Explorer"

1171 All empty souls tend to extreme opinion.
— William Butler Yeats,
Dramatis Personae, 1936

1172 After all it is setting a high value upon our opinions to roast men and women alive on account of them.
— Michel Eyquem de Montaigne, *Essays,* 1580–1595,
book I, ch. 26

1173 So many men, so many opinions.
— Terence, *Phormio,*
161 B.C., line 454

1174 Nothing is good or bad but by comparison.
— Thomas Fuller,
Gnomologia, 1732, no. 3966

1175 If there's an opinion, facts will be found to support it.

—July Sproles,
Omni, May, 1979

1176 True opinions can prevail only if the facts to which they refer are known; if they are not known, false ideas are just as effective as true ones, if not a little more effective.

—Walter Lippmann,
Liberty and the News, 1920

1177 Those who glory in the good opinion of the multitude anxiously and with daily care strive, labor, and struggle to preserve their fame. For the multitude is changeable and fickle, so that fame, if it be not preserved, soon passes away.

—Baruch Spinoza,
Ethics, 1677, part IV,
proposition 58

1178 When people are least sure, they are often most dogmatic.

—John Kenneth Galbraith,
The Great Crash, 1929,
1955, ch. 10

1179 I was gratified to be able to answer promptly, and I did. I said I didn't know.

—Mark Twain,
Life on the Mississippi,
1883, ch. 6

Optimism

1180 *Future, n.* that period of time in which our affairs prosper, our friends are true and our happiness is assured.

—Ambrose Bierce,
The Devil's Dictionary, 1906

1181 Optimism: the noble temptation to see too much in everything.

—Gilbert K. Chesterton,
Kansas City Times,
July 8, 1977

1182 When someone tells you no, that is just the beginning. The art of overcoming the word no is something you must master.

—James R. Cook,
The Start-Up Entrepreneur,
1986, ch. 6

1183 During the last recession, many companies faced the future with "cautious optimism." Hardly any chose to face it with "reckless pessimism."

—Dan Danbom,
Personal Investor Magazine,
Jan., 1986

1184 Some people have built-in filters that screen out the boos and amplify the hurrahs. Those are the people who never know when they're in trouble.

—Tommy Davis, quoted by
Roger von Oech, *A Kick
in the Seat of the Pants,*
1986, "The Judge"

1185 More are taken in by hope than by cunning.
— Luc de Clapiers,
Reflections and Maxims,
ca. 1747

1186 Being an optimist after you've got everything you want doesn't count.
— Abe Martin,
Human Behavior,
Sept., 1978

1187 The optimist proclaims that we live in the best of all possible worlds; and the pessimist fears this is true.
— James Branch Cabell,
The Silver Stallion,
1926, ch. 26

1188 It is certain because it is possible.
— Tartullian,
De Carne Christi,
ca. 209, no. 5

1189 Every cloud engenders not a storm.
— William Shakespeare,
Henry VI, Part III,
1591, act V,
scene iii, line 13

1190 The place where optimism most flourishes is the lunatic asylum.
— Havelock Ellis,
The Dance of Life,
1923, ch. 3

Organization

1191 No rule is so general, which admits not some exception.
— Robert Burton,
The Anatomy of Melancholy,
1651, part I, section 2,
member 2, subsection 3

1192 In my youth I stressed freedom, and in my old age I stress order. I have made the great discovery that liberty is a product of order.
— Will Durant,
Time, Aug. 13, 1965

1193 He that is everywhere is nowhere.
— Thomas Fuller,
Gnomologia, 1732, no. 2176

1194 Every company has two organizational structures: the formal one is written on the chart; the other is the everyday living relationship of the men and women in the organization.
— Harold Geneen with
Alvin Moscow,
Managing, 1984, ch. 4

1195 The traditional organization chart has one dead giveaway. Any dotted line indicates a troublemaker and/or a serious troubled relationship.
— Robert Townsend,
Further Up the Organization,
1984, "Organization Charts:
Rigor Mortis"

1196 If standards are not formulated systematically at the top, they will be formulated haphazardly and impulsively in the field.

> —John C. Biegler, quoted by Robert W. Kent, *Money Talks,* 1985, "Control"

1197 The problem with marketing today is not just the lack of rules. The biggest problem of all is the failure to realize that one ought to have rules in the first place.

> —Al Ries and Jack Trout, *Marketing Warfare,* 1986, ch. 16

1198 The greatest disorder of the mind is to let will direct belief.

> —Louis Pasteur, quoted by René Vallery-Radot, *The Life of Pasteur,* 1927

1199 Chaos often breeds life when order breeds habit.

> —Henry Brooks Adams, *The Education of Henry Adams,* 1907, ch. 16

1200 Those who practice the same profession recognize each other instinctively; likewise those who practice the same vice.

> —Marcel Proust, *Remembrance of Things Past,* 1913–1926, volume IV, "Cities of the Plains"

1201 The manager with the in-basket problem does not yet understand that he must discipline himself to take care of activities that fail to excite him.

> —Priscilla Elfrey, *The Hidden Agenda,* 1982, ch. 1

1202 A tidy desk encourages concentration; a disheveled one is a psychological roadblock.

> —Edwin C. Bliss, *Doing It Now,* 1986, "Step 7: Establish an Action Environment"

1203 When I come upon a man who has a gleaming, empty, clear desktop, I am dealing with a fellow who is so far removed from the realities of his business that someone else is running it for him.

> —Harold Geneen, *Fortune,* Oct. 15, 1984

1204 A holding company is a thing where you hand an accomplice the goods while the policeman searches you.

> —Will Rogers, quoted by Robert W. Kent, *Money Talks,* 1985, "Business Is and Business As"

Performance

1205 *Come through, v., informal,* to be equal to a demand; meet trouble or a sudden need with success; satisfy a need.

> —Maxine Tull Boatner, J. Edward Gates, and Adam Makkai, *A Dictionary of American Idioms,* 1987

1206 If you follow baseball, compare your own performance to that of the really fine managers in the game. Recognize that this is an excellent microcosm of the situations all managers face.
— Nicholas V. Iuppa,
Management by Guilt,
1985, part 2

1207 Civilization advances by extending the number of important operations which we can perform without thinking about them.
— Alfred North Whitehead,
An Introduction to Mathematics, 1911, ch. 5

1208 When all is said and done, a company, its chief executive, and his whole management team are judged by one criterion alone — performance.
— Harold Geneen with Alvin Moscow,
Managing,
1984, ch. 2

1209 Better break your word than do worse by keeping it.
— Thomas Fuller,
Gnomologia,
1732, no. 883

1210 Most of life is routine — dull and grubby, but routine is the momentum that keeps a man going. If you wait for inspiration you'll be standing on the corner after the parade is a mile down the street.
— Ben Nicholas, quoted by Peter Potter, *All About Success*, 1988, "Beginnings"

1211 There is a proper dignity and proportion to be observed in the performance of every act of life.
— Marcus Aurelius Antoninus, *Meditations*, 2nd century A.D., book IV, no. 32

1212 Boldness in business is the first, second, and third thing.
— Thomas Fuller,
Gnomologia,
1732, no. 1006

1213 There's never time to do it right, but always time to do it over.
— John Meskimen,
Wall Street Journal,
March 14, 1974

1214 It's all right to hesitate if you then go ahead.
— Bertolt Brecht,
The Good Woman of Setzuan,
1938–1940, prologue

1215 You are never giving, nor can you ever give, enough service.
— James R. Cook,
The Start-Up Entrepreneur,
1986, ch. 2

1216 When you have performed well, the world will remember it, when everything else is forgotten. And, most importantly, so will you.
— Harold Geneen with
Alvin Moscow, *Managing,*
1984, ch. 14

1217 No people do so much harm as those who go about doing good.
— Mandell Creighton,
Life, 1904,
volume II

Pessimism

1218 *Rain on, v. phr., slang,* to bring misfortune to (someone); to complain to (someone) about one's bad luck.
— Maxine Tull Boatner, J.
Edward Gates and Adam
Makkai, *A Dictionary of
American Idioms,* 1987

1219 No human thing is of serious importance.
— Plato, *The Republic,*
ca. 370 B.C., book X,
section 604

1220 I'd rather be seen of little skill
Than deeply learned in prophesying ill.
— Aeschylus,
The Suppliant Maidens,
ca. 490 B.C., line 453

1221 When you fully understand the situation, it is worse than you think.
— Barry Commoner
Life, Dec., 1979

1222 Every day, in every way, things are getting worse and worse.
— William F. Buckley,
National Review,
July 2, 1963

1223 Life — the way it really is — is a battle not between Bad and Good, but between Bad and Worse.
— Joseph Brodsky,
New York Times,
Oct. 1, 1972

1224 They are ill discoverers that think there is no land, when they can see nothing but sea.
— Francis Bacon,
Advancement of Learning,
1605, book II, ch. vii,
paragraph 5

1225 A device selected from random from a group having 99 percent reliability will be a member of the 1 percent group.
— Robert K. Mueller,
Board Life,
1974, ch. 11

1226 Paper is always strongest at the perforations.
— Carolyn M. Corry,
Omni, May, 1979

1227 If a project requires *n* components, there will be *n* – 1 units in stock.
— Robert K. Mueller,
Board Life,
1974, ch. 11

1228 Blessed is he who expects nothing, for he shall never be disappointed.
— Alexander Pope,
letter, Oct. 16, 1927

Planning

1229 The beginning is the most important part of any work.
— Plato, *The Republic,*
ca. 370 B.C., book II,
section 377

1230 Look with favor upon a bold beginning.
— Virgil, *Georgics I,*
ca. 30 B.C., line 40

1231 To develop and communicate a strategy, a unified sense of direction to which all members of the organization can relate, is probably the most important concept in management for top level consideration, and yet it is frequently overlooked.
— Joel E. Ross and
Michael J. Kami, *Corporate Management in Crisis: Why the Mighty Fall,* 1973, ch. 1

1232 It is a bad plan that admits no modification.
— Publilius Syrus, *Maxims,*
1st century B.C., no. 469

1233 If you do not think about the future, you cannot have one.
— John Galsworthy,
Swan Song, 1928,
part II, chapter 6

1234 Make no little plans: they have no magic to stir men's blood . . . Make big plans, aim high in hope and work.
— Daniel H. Burnham,
Christian Science Monitor,
Jan. 18, 1927

1235 A danger foreseen is half avoided.
— Thomas Fuller,
Gnomologia,
1732, no. 67

1236 Rash indeed is he who reckons on the morrow, or haply on days beyond it; for tomorrow is not, until today is safely past.
— Sophocles,
Trachiniae,
ca. 430 B.C., line 943

1237 What is the use of running when we are not on the right road?
— German proverb

1238 History is a vast early warning system.
— Norman Cousins,
Saturday Review,
April 15, 1978

1239 If you don't know where you are going, you will probably end up somewhere else.
— Laurence J. Peter,
San Francisco Chronicle,
Jan. 29, 1978

1240 The shortest distance between two points is under construction.
— Noelie Alito,
Omni, May, 1979

1241 If you can look into the seeds of time,
And say which grain will grow and which will not.
Speak then to me.
— William Shakespeare,
Macbeth, 1606, act I,
scene iii, line 58

1242 The reason why everybody likes planning is because nobody has to do anything.
— Edmund G. Brown, Jr.,
The Coevolution Quarterly,
Summer, 1976

1243 Good plans shape good decisions. That's why good planning helps to make elusive business dreams come true.
— Lester R. Bittel,
The Nine Master Keys
of Management, 1972, ch. 5

1244 Poor execution of planning principles will always be the result of a traditional approach which focuses on the process instead of on the system in which planning and doing are taking place.
— William C. Waddell,
Overcoming Murphy's
Law, 1981, ch. 1

1245 Modern industry needs visionary heroes more than ever before, not only to build new worlds but also to invent better mousetraps.
— Terrence E. Deal and
Allen A. Kennedy,
Corporate Cultures,
1982, ch. 3

1246 The trouble with research is that it tells you what people were thinking about yesterday, not tomorrow. It's like driving a car using a rear-view mirror.
— Bernard Loomis,
International Herald
Tribune, Oct. 9, 1985

1247 A sensible man never embarks on an enterprise until he can see his way clear to the end of it.
— Aesop, fable,
"Look Before You Leap,"
ca. 550 B.C.

1248 Maybe you can *start* a company without knowing how to plan — but if you don't learn,

sooner or later you'll pay an enormous price.
— Bruce G. Posner,
Inc. Magazine,
Nov., 1985

1249 A good manager is eternally dissatisfied. He is always looking for a better way to perform. The effective manager continually asks, "Am I doing this job in the best way, or is there a better way to do it?"
— Ronald Brown,
The Practical Manager's Guide to Excellence in Management, 1979, ch. 9

1250 Planning is but another word for the vision that sees a creative achievement before it is manifest. Control is·but a name for direction.
— James L. Pierce,
Harvard Business Review, 1954

1251 When there is no vision, the people perish.
— Bible, Proverbs 29:18

1252 He knew the things that were and the things that would be and the things that had been before.
— Homer, *The Iliad,*
ca. 550 B.C.,
book I, line 70

1253 Beyond the loathing and the fear lies one of the best-kept secrets in American

business. "Planning," it turns out, is really no more — and no less — than another word for good management.
— Bruce G. Posner,
Inc. Magazine,
Nov., 1985

1254 Business more than any other occupation is a continual dealing with the future; it is a continual calculation, an instinctive exercise in foresight.
— Henry R. Luce,
Fortune,
Oct., 1960

1255 Strategic planning is worthless — unless there is first a strategic vision.
— John Naisbitt,
Megatrends,
1984, ch. 4

1256 For the happiest life, days should be rigorously planned, nights left open to chance.
— Mignon McLaughlin,
Atlantic,
July, 1965

1257 The first prerequisite of intelligent tinkering is to save all the pieces.
— Aldo Leopold,
Washingtonian,
Sept., 1978

1258 The entire management function revolves around

accepted objectives and the strategy for reaching them.

— Ronald Brown,
The Practical Manager's Guide to Excellence in Management, 1979, ch. 3

1259 Managing means that once you set your business plan and budget for the year, you *must* achieve the sales, the market share, and the earnings to which you committed yourself. If you don't manage to achieve those results, you're not a manager.

— Harold Geneen,
Fortune, Oct. 1, 1984

1260 Life is what happens while you are making other plans.

— John Lennon, quoted by Robert Byrne,
The 637 Best Things Anybody Ever Said, 1982, no. 31

Power

1261 It does not do to leave a live dragon out of your calculations, if you live near him.

— J.R.R. Tolkien,
Reader's Digest, Sept., 1978

1262 'Tis the sorest of all human ills, to abound in knowledge and yet have no power over action.

— Herodotus, *The History,*
ca. 450 B.C., book IX, ch. 16

1263 Except our own thoughts, there is nothing absolutely in our power.

— René Descartes,
Discourse on the Method,
1637, part III

1264 The acquisition chain letter can't go on forever. Geometric growth through acquisition gets increasingly difficult. If this were not so, a handful of conglomerates would own the entire country.

— Joel E. Ross and Michael J. Kami, *Corporate Management in Crisis: Why the Mighty Fall,* 1973, ch. 6

1265 The dinosaur's eloquent lesson is that if some bigness is good, an overabundance of bigness is not necessarily better.

— Eric Johnston,
Quote Magazine,
Feb. 23, 1958

1266 The big-business mergers and the big-labor mergers have all the appearance of dinosaurs mating.

— John Naisbitt,
Megatrends, 1984, ch. 4

1267 The power of the executive is like a chess game; there are very few moves that one can make.

— Edmund G. Brown, Jr.,
Gold Coast Pictorial,
Feb., 1977

1268 I have seen the wicked in great power, and spreading himself like a green bay tree.
—Bible, Psalm 37:35

1269 Where the will to power is wanting, there is decline.
—Friedrich Nietzsche,
The Anti-Christ,
1888, aphorism 6

1270 For the crowd, the incredible has sometimes more power and is more credible than truth.
—Menander,
Fragment 622,
3rd century B.C.

1271 The more noise a man or a motor makes the less power there is available.
—W.R. McGeary, quoted by Peter Potter,
All About Success,
1988, "Acquiring Power"

1272 Loudness is impotence.
—Johann Kaspar Lavater,
Aphorisms on Man, 1788

1273 Force without wisdom falls of its own weight.
—Horace, *Epodes III,*
ca. 25 B.C.,
stanza IV, line 65

1274 Immense power is acquired by assuring yourself in your secret reveries that you were born to control affairs.
—Andrew Carnegie, quoted by Peter Potter,
All About Success,
1988, "Acquiring Power"

1275 The majority has the might—more's the pity—but it hasn't right. The minority is always right.
—Henrik Ibsen,
An Enemy of the People,
1882, act IV

1276 Physical strength can never permanently withstand the impact of spiritual force.
—Franklin D. Roosevelt,
speech, May 4, 1941

1277 The desire for glory clings even to the best men longer than any other passion.
—Cornelius Tacitus,
The Histories, ca. A.D. 95,
book IV, ch. 6

1278 The very essence of all power lies in getting the other person to participate.
—Harry Overstreet, quoted by Zig Ziglar, *Secrets of Closing the Sale,*
1984, ch. 29

1279 I really believe that more harm is done by old men who cling to their influence than by young men who anticipate it.
—Owen D. Young,
New York Herald Tribune,
July 12, 1962

Problems

1280 A problem is something you have hopes of changing. Anything else is a fact of life.
— C.R. Smith,
Publishers Weekly,
Sept. 8, 1969

1281 Worry, the interest paid by those who borrow trouble.
— George W. Lyon,
New York Times Book Review, Oct. 23, 1932

1282 In my experience, the worst thing you can do to an important problem is discuss it.
— Simon Gray, quoted by Robert W. Kent,
Money Talks, 1985,
"Communications"

1283 Nothing is easy to the unwilling.
— Thomas Fuller,
Gnomologia,
1732, no. 3663

1284 Intractable problems are usually not intractable because there are no solutions, but because there are no solutions without severe side effects.
— Lester C. Thurow,
The Zero-Sum Society, 1980

1285 The certainties of one age are the problems of the next.
— Richard H. Tawney,
Religion and the Rise of Capitalism,
1926, ch. 5

1286 People who are only good with hammers see every problem as a nail.
— Abraham Maslow, quoted by Roger von Oech, *A Kick in the Seat of the Pants,* 1986, "The Explorer"

1287 Almost anything is easier to get into than to get out of.
— Agnes Allen,
Omni, May, 1979

1288 All things are difficult before they are easy.
— Thomas Fuller,
Gnomologia,
1732, no. 560

1289 When politicians come up with a solution to your problem, you have two problems.
— J. Kesner Kahn,
American Opinion,
May, 1975

1290 Problems increase in geometric ratio, solutions in arithmetic ratio.
— Charles Issawi,
The Columbia Forum,
Summer, 1970

1291 Any solution to a problem changes the problem.
— Robert W. Johnson,
Washingtonian,
Nov., 1979

1292 The chief cause of problems is solutions.
— Eric Sevareid,
Reader's Digest,
March, 1974

1293 Management is 85% of the problem.
— W. Edwards Deming,
quoted by Robert W. Kent,
Money Talks,
1985, "Managers"

1294 Management calls upon a person to brace himself for the long haul. He must cope again and again with problems that are substantially technical, as well as with pressures that are increasingly emotional.
— Lester R. Bittel,
The Nine Master Keys of Management, 1972, ch. 9

1295 I have yet to see any problem, however complicated, which, when you looked at it in the right way, did not become still more complicated.
— Paul Anderson,
Washingtonian,
Nov., 1978

1296 Management by exception is the golden technique by which a manager applies lever-age to the mountain of problems and opportunities that challenge his daily existence.
— Lester R. Bittel,
The Nine Master Keys of Management, 1972, ch. 6

1297 When all else fails, read the instructions.
— Agnes Allen,
Omni, May, 1979

Procrastination

1298 Procrastination is the thief of time.
— Edward Young,
Night Thoughts,
1742, "Night I," line 393

1299 Defer no time, delays have dangerous ends.
— William Shakespeare,
Henry VI, Part I,
1591, act III,
scene ii, line 33

1300 Delay is preferable to error.
— Thomas Jefferson,
letter, May 16, 1792

1301 Never let the difficulty of a task stand as an adequate reason for not acting; force yourself to identify precisely what is to be gained in the long run by delay. In most cases you'll find you can't.
— Edwin C. Bliss, *Doing It Now,* 1986, "Step 12: Learn to Deal with the Top Forty Cop-Outs"

1302 What may be done at any time will be done at no time.
— Thomas Fuller,
Gnomologia,
1732, no. 5500

1303 When people have a job to do, particularly a vital but difficult one, they will invariably put it off until the last possible moment, and most of them will put it off even longer.
— Gordon Becker,
Wall Street Journal,
Feb. 26, 1976

1304 Properly used, a pencil can be one of the most effective weapons against procrastination.
— Edwin C. Bliss,
Doing It Now, 1986,
"Step 2: Develop a Game Plan"

1305 Hope deferred maketh the heart sick.
— Bible, Proverbs 13:12

Productivity

1306 You can never do merely one thing.
— Garrett Hardin,
Fortune,
Feb., 1973

1307 You begin well in nothing except you end well.
— Thomas Fuller,
Gnomologia,
1732, no. 5863

1308 Filing is concerned with the past; anything you actually need to see again has to do with the future.
— Katharine Whitehorn,
quoted by Robert W. Kent,
Money Talks, 1985,
"Production and Operations"

1309 If you want work well done, select a busy man: the other kind has no time.
— Elbert Hubbard,
The Note Book, 1927

1310 A really busy person never knows how much he weighs.
— Edgar Watson Howe,
Country Town Sayings, 1911

1311 The big unions served a noble purpose once, and bless them for it. Now they're part of the problem and must give way if America is to move into participative management and achieve reasonable productivity.
— Robert Townsend,
*Further Up the
Organization,* 1984,
"Big Labor Unions: Sounds of the Dying Dinosaur"

1312 Example is always more efficacious than precept.
— Samuel Johnson,
Rasselas,
1759, ch. 29

Profit

1313 To contract new debts is not the way to pay old ones.
— George Washington,
letter,
April 7, 1799

1314 Net — the biggest word in the language of business.
— Herbert Casson, quoted by Robert W. Kent,
Money Talks,
1985, "Control"

1315 Prudent investor: someone who made money in the third quarter, 1986.
— Kurt Brouwer,
Unusual Investment Definitions, 1987

1316 Never invest your money in anything that eats or needs repainting.
— Billy Rose,
New York Post,
Oct. 26, 1957

1317 Getting money is like digging with a needle. Spending it is like water soaking into sand.
— Japanese proverb

1318 The best plan is to profit by the folly of others.
— Pliny the Elder,
Natural History,
ca. A.D. 75, book XVIII,
section 31

1319 He was a gentleman who was generally spoken of as having nothing a-year, paid quarterly.
— R.S. Surtees,
Mr. Sponge's Sporting Tour,
1853, ch. 24

1320 The happiest time in any man's life is when he is in red-hot pursuit of a dollar with a reasonable prospect of overtaking it.
— Henry Wheeler Shaw,
quoted by Robert W. Kent,
Money Talks, 1985,
"Entrepreneurs"

1321 A prudent mind can see room for misgiving, lest he who prospers should one day suffer reverse.
— Sophocles, *Trachiniae,*
ca. 430 B.C., line 296

1322 The proper man understands equity, the small man profits.
— Confucius,
Analects, ca. 500 B.C.,
book IV, ch. 6

1323 Businessmen commit a fraud when they say they're interested in anything but profit.
— Jim Brooks,
New West,
Dec. 20, 1976

1324 He made his money the really old-fashioned way. He inherited it.
— A.J. Carothers, *The Secret of My Success,* 1987

1325 In business, there is no bottom of the ninth, one-yard line, or double overtime. And you certainly never get a two-minute warning.
— Nicholas V. Iuppa, *Management by Guilt,* 1985, part 2

1326 Customer satisfaction is key to long-term profitability and keeping the customer happy is *everybody's* business.
— Milind M. Lele with Jagdish N. Sheth, *The Customer Is Key,* 1987, preface

1327 The easiest job I have ever tackled in this world is that of making money. It is, in fact, almost as easy as losing it. Almost, but not quite.
— H.L. Mencken, *Baltimore Evening Sun,* June 12, 1922

1328 Ultimately, vision gets translated into sales and profit growth and return on investment, but the numbers come after the vision. In the old-style companies, the numbers are the vision.
— John Naisbitt and Patricia Aburdene, *Re-inventing the Corporation,* 1985, ch. 1

1329 Where profit is, loss hides nearby.
— Japanese proverb

1330 There are occasions when it is undoubtedly better to incur loss than to make gain.
— Titus Maccius Plautus, *Captivi,* ca. 200 B.C., act II, scene ii, line 77

Progress

1331 Progress is what happens when impossibility yields to necessity.
— Arnold H. Glasow, quoted by Peter Potter, *All About Success,* 1988, "Progress"

1332 The true joy and reward of entrepreneurial life are the freedom and exhilaration of the new venture dream.
— Deaver Brown, *The Entrepreneur's Guide,* 1980, ch. 1

1333 Like an ox-cart driver in monsoon season or the skipper of a grounded ship, one must sometimes go forward by going back.
— John Barth, *New York Times,* Sept. 16, 1984

1334 The march of the human mind is slow.
— Edmund Burke, speech, March 22, 1775

1335 Habit is habit, and not to be flung out of the window by any man, but coaxed downstairs a step at a time.
— Mark Twain,
Pudd'nhead Wilson,
1894, ch. 6

1336 Never let your mind get set — except on the objective of succeeding by exercising an open mind.
— Robert Heller,
The Super Managers,
1984, ch. 8

1337 Growth is a cultural value: a company that is not expanding is said to be falling behind. A stigma is associated with the failure to grow.
— Milton C. Lauenstein,
Harvard Business Review,
Sept.-Oct., 1984

1338 The business of life is to go forward.
— Samuel Johnson, *The Idler,*
1759, no. 72

1339 Progress might have been all right once, but it's gone on too long.
— Ogden Nash,
Reader's Digest,
Feb., 1975

1340 That's the old American way — if you get a good thing, then overdo it.
— Phil Walden,
Rolling Stone,
July 1, 1976

1341 Going to work for a large company is like getting on a train. Are you going sixty miles an hour or is the train going sixty miles an hour and you're just sitting still?
— J. Paul Getty, quoted by Robert W. Kent,
Money Talks, 1985, "Managers"

1342 Progress needs the brakeman, but the brakeman should not spend all his time putting on the brakes.
— Elbert Hubbard, quoted by Robert W. Kent,
Money Talks, 1985,
"Business and Government"

1343 Trends, like horses, are easier to ride in the direction they are already going.
— John Naisbitt,
Megatrends, 1984,
introduction

1344 Business is like riding a bicycle. Either you keep moving or you fall down.
— John David Wright,
quoted by Robert W. Kent,
Money Talks, 1985,
"Business Is and Business As"

1345 When you soar like an eagle, you attract the hunters.
— Milton S. Gould,
Time, Dec. 8, 1967

1346 In attacking, unless you have a three-to-one

advantage — and even if you
do — go around the side.
— Robert Heller,
The Super Managers,
1984, ch. 9

1347 All progress is based
upon a universal innate desire
on the part of every organism
to live beyond its income.
— Samuel Butler,
Notebooks, 1912

1348 We must beware of
needless innovations, especially
when guided by logic.
— Winston S. Churchill,
address, Dec. 17, 1942

1349 Whenever man comes
up with a better mousetrap,
nature immediately comes up
with a better mouse.
— James Carswell,
Omni, May, 1979

1350 No progress of
humanity is possible unless it
shakes off the yoke of authority
and tradition.
— André Gide, *Journal,*
March 17, 1931

1351 Most advances in
science come when a person for
one reason or another is forced
to change fields.
— Peter Borden, quoted
by Roger von Oech,
*A Whack on the Side
of the Head,* 1983, "Breaktime"

1352 Where I am today has
everything to do with the years
I spent hanging on by my
fingernails.
— Barbara Aronstein Black,
New York Times,
Jan. 2, 1986

Quality

1353 *Brummagem, adj.* phony,
cheap. — *n.* something cheap or
gaudy, especially phony jewelry
(slang from Birmingham,
England, where cheap gift
items, primarily jewelry, were
made).
— Josefa Heifetz Bryne,
Mrs. Byrne's Dictionary, 1974

1354 Nothing so rivets the
attention of employees as
discussions of quality, and
nothing will get results from
those discussions except
managerial insistence that standards be met.
— Woodrow H. Sears, Jr.,
Back in Working Order,
1984, ch. 3

1355 With productivity, you
can march to the beat of your
own drum; but, when it comes
to quality, you'd better get in
step. Otherwise, you'll find that
you're a downsized drummer.
— Jeffrey G. Allen,
*Surviving Corporate
Downsizing,* 1988, ch. 7

1356 Business is many things, the least of which is the balance sheet.
— Harold Geneen with Alvin Moscow, *Managing,* 1984, preface

1357 Not one tenth of us who are in business are doing as well as we could if we merely followed the principles that were known to our grandfathers.
— William Feather, quoted by Robert W. Kent, *Money Talks,* 1985, "Business Is and Business As"

1358 By the work one knows the workman.
— Jean de la Fontaine, *Fables,* book I, 1668, fable 21

1359 What is not good at the beginning cannot be rendered good by time.
— The Universal Self-Instructor, 1883, "Legal Maxims"

1360 Nothing is so good that some fault cannot be found with it.
— Aesop, fable, "Room for Improvement," ca. 550 B.C.

1361 'So-so' is good, very good, very excellent good: and yet it is not; it is but so so.
— William Shakespeare, *As You Like It,* 1600, act V, scene i, line 30

1362 There is a crack in everything God has made.
— Ralph Waldo Emerson, *Essays: First Series,* 1841, "Compensation"

Questions and Answers

1363 It's a healthy thing now and then to hang a question mark on the things you have long taken for granted.
— Bertrand Russell, quoted by Peter Potter, *All About Success,* 1988, "Doubt"

1364 You see things; and you say, "Why?" But I dream things that never were; and I say, "Why not?"
— George Bernard Shaw, *Back to Methuselah,* 1921, part I, act I

1365 If you don't ask "why this?" often enough, somebody will ask "why you?"
— Tim Hirshfield, quoted by Roger von Oech, *A Kick in the Seat of the Pants,* 1986, "The Artist"

1366 The first key to wisdom is this — constant and frequent questioning ... for by doubting we are led to questions and by questioning we arrive at the truth.
— Pierre Abélard, *Sic et Non,* ca. 1120, prologue

1367 A competent professional listens well, probes, asks questions, and thinks before he speaks. This is easy to say, but hard to do.
—Jeffrey G. Allen,
*Surviving Corporate
Downsizing,* 1988, ch. 1

1368 It is better to know some of the questions than all of the answers.
—James Thurber, quoted
by Robert W. Kent,
Money Talks, 1985,
"Microeconomics"

1369 Life is made up of constant calls to action, and we seldom have time for more than hastily contrived answers.
—Learned Hand,
speech, Jan. 27, 1952

1370 It is not the answer that enlightens, but the question.
—Eugene Ionesco,
Découvertes, 1969

1371 For an answer which cannot be expressed the question too cannot be expressed.
—Ludwig Wittenstein,
*Tractatus Logico—
Philosophicus,* 1922

1372 Asking the right questions takes as much skill as giving the right answers.
—Robert Half,
Robert Half on Hiring,
1985, ch. 7

1373 'Tis not every question that deserves an answer.
—Thomas Fuller,
Gnomologia,
1732, no. 5094

1374 Good questions outrank easy answers.
—Paul A. Samuelson,
Newsweek, Aug. 21, 1978

1375 The only interesting answers are those which destroy the questions.
—Susan Sontag,
Esquire, July, 1968

Reality

1376 Contrary to popular belief, a manager's success often depends upon the degree to which he can be cynical, skeptical, and conservative. While a general sense of optimism is essential, a manager's sense of harsh reality is his trump card.
—Lester R. Bittel,
*The Nine Master Keys of
Management,* 1972, ch. 3

1377 It is time that financial types developed a greater tolerance for imprecision, because that's the way the world is.
—John C. Burton,
Time, Jan. 24, 1977

1378 Farming looks mighty easy when your plow is a pencil

and you're a thousand miles from a cornfield.
— Dwight D. Eisenhower, speech, Sept. 25, 1956

1379 Don't get rich with a pencil. Visions of high sales and high profits that are forecast without adequate planning seldom come to pass. Be careful of seducing yourself.
— Joel E. Ross and Michael J. Kami, *Corporate Management in Crisis: Why the Mighty Fall,* 1973, ch. 2

1380 The great majority of mankind are satisfied with appearances, as though they were realities and are often more influenced by the things that seem than by those that are.
— Niccolò Machiavelli, *Discourses on the First Ten Books of Titus Livius,* 1513–1517, book I, ch. 25

1381 Instinct can be invaluable in running a business so long as it is soundly based on reality. Unfortunately, not every executive who plays his hunches is able to muster the basic soundness that makes the approach work.
— Henry O. Golightly, *Managing with Style,* 1977, ch. 2

1382 An idealist believes the short run doesn't count. A cynic believes the long run doesn't

matter. A realist believes that what is done or left undone in the short run determines the long run.
— Sydney J. Harris, *Reader's Digest,* May, 1979

1383 We live in a fantasy world, a world of illusion. The great task in life is to find reality.
— Iris Murdoch, *Times of London,* April 15, 1983

Recognition

1384 *Pat on the back, v. phr.* 1. to clap lightly on the back in support, encouragement, or praise. 2. to make your support or encouragement for (someone) felt; praise.
— Maxine Tull Boatner, J. Edward Gates, and Adam Makkai, *A Dictionary of American Idioms,* 1987

1385 Every other author may aspire to praise; the lexicographer can only hope to escape reproach.
— Samuel Johnson, *Dictionary of the English Language,* 1775, preface

1386 Whereas the well-functioning executive encourages the best brains and skills, the one who is paranoid

127

or even less morbidly insecure must have inadequates about him, men who will take punishment.
— Francis J. Braceland,
National Observer,
Dec. 28, 1964

1387 All resources are not obvious; great managers find and develop available talent.
— Zig Ziglar,
Top Performance,
1982, ch. 2

1388 The only way I can compete with larger corporations is to treat my employees better, move them up faster, give them more money and put mirrors in the bathroom.
— James R. Uffelman,
Wall Street Journal,
Aug. 21, 1984

1389 Open thou my lips; and my mouth shall show forth thy praise.
— Bible, Psalm 51:15

1390 Praise makes good men better and bad men worse.
— Thomas Fuller,
Gnomologia,
1732, no. 3924

1391 Money is not so important as a pat on the head.
— C.P. Snow,
The Observer,
Dec. 18, 1977

1392 So is a word better than a gift.
— Bible: Apocrypha,
Ecclesiasticus 18:16

1393 There is no such whetstone, to sharpen a good wit and encourage a will to learning, as is praise.
— Roger Ascham,
The Schoolmaster,
1570, part I

1394 Employee motivation is a complex science, but its foundations rest on the simple recognition that we all need to feel important in some phase of our lives.
— Terrence E. Deal and
Allen A. Kennedy,
Corporate Cultures,
1982, ch. 3

1395 The purpose of organizations is to help people have lives. Lives come from the challenges and support that people derive from being responsible, being supplied, or being cared for.
— Philip B. Crosby,
Running Things,
1986, ch. 1

1396 The wretched souls of those who lived without infamy and without praise maintain this miserable mode.
— Dante, *The Divine Comedy,*
ca. 1315, "Inferno,"
canto III, line 34

1397 Popularity? It is glory's small change.
— Victor Hugo,
Ruy Blas, 1838,
act III, scene v

Reports

1398 Cut the paperwork associated with controls. A system will break down fast when reports become the end instead of the means.
— Joel E. Ross and
Michael J. Kami, *Corporate Management in Crisis: Why the Mighty Fall,* 1973, ch. 12

1399 Annual reports are the product of having English majors write about complicated and sometimes embarrassing financial matters and having accountants write about anything at all.
— Dan Danbom,
Personal Investor Magazine,
Jan., 1986

1400 The annual report is a company's number one public relations tool.
— Robert Dallos,
Personal Investor Magazine,
April, 1985

1401 I don't read the president's message in an annual report. I just look at his picture.

If he's smiling too hard, I know the company's in big trouble.
— Michael C. Thomsett,
A Treasury of Business Quotations, 1990, page 129

1402 "White space" is a designer term for "nothing," and last year alone, designers charged American companies $6 million just for the white space they put in their annual reports.
— Dan Danbom,
Personal Investor Magazine,
Jan., 1986

1403 It shall be a vexation only to understand the report.
— Bible, Isaiah 28:19

Responsibility

1404 *Hypengyophobia, n.* fear of responsibility.
— Josefa Heifetz Byrne,
Mrs. Byrne's Dictionary, 1974

1405 *Corporation, n.* an ingenious device for obtaining individual profit without individual responsibility.
— Ambrose Bierce,
The Devil's Dictionary, 1906

1406 Like the Church, companies also have priests. They are the designated worriers of the corporation and the

guardians of the culture's values.
— Terrence E. Deal and Allen A. Kennedy, *Corporate Cultures,* 1982, ch. 5

1407 Everyone is really responsible to all men for all men and for everything.
— Fyodor Dostoyevski, *The Brothers Karamazov,* 1880, part II, book VI

1408 I believe that every right implies a responsibility; every opportunity an obligation; every possession, a duty.
— John D. Rockefeller, speech, July 8, 1941

1409 When I've had a rough day, before I go to sleep I ask myself if there's anything more I can do right now. If there isn't, I sleep sound.
— L.L. Colbert, *Newsweek,* Aug. 22, 1955

1410 A councilor ought not to sleep the whole night through, a man to whom the populace is entrusted, and who has many responsibilities.
— Homer, *The Iliad,* ca. 550 B.C., book II, line 24

1411 I believe that all of us have the capacity for one adventure inside us, but great adventure is facing responsibility day after day.
— William Gordon, *Time,* Nov. 19, 1965

1412 Throughout history, those in power have been more willing to allow access to the process, procedures, etiquettes, forms, meetings, and councils than they have been to change the structure that would free people to take on the substance of higher responsibility.
— Frederick Herzberg, *The Managerial Choice: To Be Efficient and to Be Human,* 1982

1413 Employees must be given responsibility; to be backed with investment; and to be provided with motivation. Good people won't stay without them.
— Robert Heller, *The Super Managers,* 1984, ch. 9

1414 Man is not like other animals in the ways that are really significant: animals have instincts, we have taxes.
— Erving Goffman, *New York Times,* Feb. 12, 1969

1415 None knows the weight of another's burden.
— Thomas Fuller, *Gnomologia,* 1732, no. 3655

Risk

1416 When written in Chinese, the word *crisis* is

composed of two characters. One represents danger and the other represents opportunity.
—John F. Kennedy, speech, April 12, 1959

1417 The market doesn't reward qualities that are not scarce.
—Mark A. Johnson, *The Random Walk and Beyond*, 1988, ch. 1

1418 To conquer without risk is to triumph without glory.
—Pierre Corneille, *Le Cid*, 1636, act II, scene ii

1419 If the creator had a purpose in equipping us with a neck, he surely would have meant for us to stick it out.
—Arthur Koestler, quoted by Roger von Oech, *A Kick in the Seat of the Pants*, 1986, "The Warrior"

1420 Everyone has a "risk muscle." You keep it in shape by trying new things. If you don't, it atrophies. Make a point of using it at least once a day.
—Roger von Oech, *A Kick in the Seat of the Pants*, 1986, "The Warrior"

1421 The greater the "risk," usually the worse the idea.
—Robert Heller, *The Super Managers*, 1984, ch. 8

1422 Today, the man who is the real risk-taker is anonymous and nonheroic. He is the one trying to make institutions work.
—John William Ward, *Time*, Nov. 17, 1955

1423 A ship in port is safe, but that's not what ships are built for.
—Grace Murray Hopper, quoted by Roger von Oech, *A Kick in the Seat of the Pants*, 1986, "The Judge"

1424 He that will not sail till all dangers are over must never put to sea.
—Thomas Fuller, *Gnomologia*, 1732, no. 2353

1425 Take calculated risks. That is quite different from being rash.
—George S. Patton, letter, June 6, 1944

1426 Better hazard once than always be in fear.
—Thomas Fuller, *Gnomologia*, 1732, no. 906

1427 Considering how dangerous everything is, nothing is really frightening.
—Gertrude Stein, quoted in *Human Behavior*, May, 1978

1428 If you play it safe in life, you've decided that you don't want to grow anymore.
— Shirley Hufstedler, quoted by Peter Potter, *All About Success,* 1988, "Boldness"

1429 No one ever achieved greatness by playing it safe.
— Harry Gray, quoted by Roger von Oech, *A Kick in the Seat of the Pants,* 1986, "The Judge"

1430 There is no safety in numbers, or in anything else.
— James Thurber, *Washingtonian,* Nov., 1978

1431 The real risk is doing nothing.
— Denis Waitley and Remi L. Witt, *The Joy of Working,* 1985, "Day 18, Risk Taking"

1432 The key to success in the risk/return game is not to minimize or maximize risk, but to manage it.
— Mark A. Johnson, *The Random Walk and Beyond,* 1988, ch. 7

1433 The chief danger in life is that you may take too many precautions.
— Alfred Adler, *Kansas City Times,* Jan. 24, 1977

1434 You can't make an omelet without breaking eggs.
— French proverb

1435 Two dangers constantly threaten the world: order and disorder.
— Paul Valéry, *The Nation,* Jan. 5, 1957

1436 Nothing in life is so exhilarating as to be shot at without result.
— Winston S. Churchill, quoted by Robert W. Kent, *Money Talks,* 1985, "Bottom Line"

Security

1437 The past at least is secure.
— Daniel Webster, speech, Jan. 26, 1830

1438 There are one hundred men seeking security to one able man who is willing to risk his fortune.
— J. Paul Getty, *International Herald Tribune,* Jan. 10, 1961

1439 The worse the passage the more welcome the port.
— Thomas Fuller, *Gnomologia,* 1732, no. 4848

1440 Lip service strategy is worse than none, because it lulls management into a false sense of security.
—Joel E. Ross and Michael J. Kami, *Corporate Management in Crisis: Why the Mighty Fall,* 1973, ch. 10

1441 He who is firmly seated in authority soon learns to think security, and not progress.
—James Russell Lowell, *Among My Books,* 1870

1442 Don't lull yourself into a false state of security by engaging your skills for a week or two and then abandoning them. It's what you do every day on the job that counts.
—Warren H. Reed, *Savvy* Magazine, Jan., 1986

1443 He that is too secure is not safe.
—Thomas Fuller, *Gnomologia,* 1732, no. 2195

1444 Security is when everything is settled, when nothing can happen to you; security is a denial of life.
—Germaine Greer, *Redbook,* March, 1977

1445 Security is a kind of death.
—Tennessee Williams, *Esquire* Magazine, Sept., 1971

Self-Esteem

1446 Accountants are perpetually fighting their shiny pants, green eyeshades, number-cruncher image.
—Albert Newgarden, *Wall Street Journal,* April 26, 1984

1447 How many cares one loses when one decides not to be something, but to be someone.
—Gabrielle Chanel, *This Week,* Aug. 20, 1961

1448 Every man's work, whether it be literature or music or pictures or architecture or anything else, is always a portrait of himself.
—Samuel Butler, *The Way of All Flesh,* 1903, ch. 14

1449 If we had no faults of our own, we would not take so much pleasure in noticing those of others.
—François, Duc de la Rochefoucauld, *Reflections; or, Sentences and Moral Maxims,* 1665, maxim 31

1450 There can be no progress in the workplace until an individual values himself and feels valued by others. That's

the foundation of all human ful-
fillment.
— Denis Waitley and
Remi L. Witt, *The Joy of
Working,* 1985, prologue

1451 For workaholics, all the
eggs of self-esteem are in the
basket of work.
— Judith M. Bardwick,
The Plateauing Trap,
1988, ch. 6

1452 "You're fired!" No
other words can so easily and
succinctly reduce a confident,
self-assured executive to an insecure, groveling shred of his
former self.
— Frank P. Louchheim,
Wall Street Journal,
July 16, 1984

1453 Real confidence comes
from knowing and accepting
yourself — your strengths and
your limitations — in contrast to
depending on affirmation from
others, from outside.
— Judith M. Bardwick,
The Plateauing Trap,
1988, ch. 8

1454 Every new adjustment
is a crisis in self-esteem.
— Eric Hoffer, *The Ordeal
of Change,* 1963

1455 Of all the traps and
pitfalls in life, self-disesteem is
the deadliest, and the hardest to
overcome, for it is a pit designed

and dug by our own hands,
summed up in the phrase, "It's
no use — I can't do it."
— Maxwell Maltz,
This Week, July 24, 1955

1456 The essential element
in personal magnetism is a con-
suming sincerity — an overwhelming faith in the importance of the work one has to do.
— Bruce Barton,
quoted by Peter Potter,
All About Success,
1988, "Conviction"

1457 If you view yourself as
an impartial, tough-minded,
money-motivated, bottom-line-
oriented manager, you probably
will not receive the pleasures
from new venture life to sustain
you through its bleakest hours.
— Deaver Brown,
The Entrepreneur's Guide,
1980, ch. 2

1458 The mathematics of
self-pity can be raised to
infinity.
— Cornelius Ryan,
Time, Aug. 6, 1979

Selling

1459 Selling is essentially a
transference of feeling.
— Zig Ziglar,
Secrets of Closing the Sale,
1984, ch. 7

1460 Nothing ever happens until somebody sells something.
— Richard M. White, Jr.,
The Entrepreneur's Manual,
1977, ch. 16

1461 The value of anything is not what you get paid for it, nor what it cost to produce, but what you can get for it at an auction.
— William Lyon Phelps,
National Observer, 1969

1462 There is no such thing as "soft sell" and "hard sell." There is only "smart sell" and "stupid sell."
— Charles Brower,
news summaries,
May 20, 1958

1463 Some corporate employees spend years without ever meeting a customer or seeing a competitive salesperson. These are the "cooks and the bakers" of corporate America.
— Al Ries and Jack Trout,
Marketing Warfare,
1986, ch. 10

1464 You can learn a lot from the client . . . some 70 percent doesn't matter, but that 30 percent will kill you.
— Paul J. Paulson,
New York Times,
May 4, 1979

1465 Strategy should evolve out of the mud of the market-place, not in the antiseptic environment of an ivory tower.
— Al Ries and Jack Trout,
Marketing Warfare,
1986, ch. 15

1466 We are all salesmen every day of our lives. We are selling our ideas, our plans, our enthusiasms to those with whom we come in contact.
— Charles M. Schwab,
quoted by Peter Potter,
All About Success,
1988, "Selling"

1467 Never underestimate the power of the irate customer.
— Joel E. Ross and Michael J. Kami, *Corporate Management in Crisis: Why the Mighty Fall,* 1973, ch. 9

1468 Advertising is what you do when you can't go see somebody. That's all it is.
— Fairfax Cone,
Christian Science Monitor,
March 20, 1963

1469 Advertising is a valuable economic factor because it is the cheapest way of selling goods, particularly if the goods are worthless.
— Sinclair Lewis,
New York Times,
April 18, 1943

1470 The first law in advertising is to avoid the concrete

promise . . . and cultivate the delightfully vague.
—John Crosby,
New York Herald Tribune,
Aug. 18, 1947

1471 You make the sale when the prospect understands that it will cost more to do nothing about the problem than to do something about it.
— Ben Feldman, quoted by Zig Ziglar, *Secrets of Closing the Sale,*
1984, ch. 20

1472 All media exist to invest our lives with artificial perceptions and arbitrary values.
— Marshall McLuhan,
Understanding Media: The Extensions of Man,
1964, part II, ch. 20

1473 Advertising may be described as the science of arresting the human intelligence long enough to get money from it.
— Stephen Leacock, quoted by Robert W. Kent,
Money Talks,
1985, "Marketing"

1474 Strategy and timing are the Himalayas of marketing. Everything else is the Catskills.
— Al Ries and Jack Trout,
Marketing Warfare,
1986, ch. 16

1475 The meek have to inherit the earth—they sure don't know how to market it.
—Jeno F. Palucci,
New York Times,
Nov. 7, 1976

Silence

1476 *Clam up, v., slang,* to refuse to say anything more; stop talking.
—Maxine Tull Boatner, J. Edward Gates, and Adam Makkai, *A Dictionary of American Idioms,* 1987

1477 Men of few words are the best men.
—William Shakespeare,
Henry V, 1600,
act III, scene ii, line 40

1478 'Tis easier to know how to speak than how to be silent.
—Thomas Fuller,
Gnomologia,
1732, no. 5075

1479 Do you wish people to believe good of you? Don't speak.
— Blaise Pascal,
Pensées, 1670, no. 44

1480 The time to stop talking is when the other person nods his head affirmatively but says nothing.
—Henry S. Haskins, quoted by Peter Potter, *All About Success,* 1988, "Selling"

1481 When you have nothing to say, say nothing.
— Charles Caleb Colton,
Lacon, 1820,
vol. I, no. 183

1482 Blessed is the man who, having nothing to say, abstains from giving in words evidence of the fact.
— George Eliot,
Impressions of Theophrastus Such,
1879

1483 When you are in it up to your ears, keep your mouth shut.
— P.L. Stewart,
Omni, May, 1979

1484 Never say more than is necessary.
— Richard Brinsley Sheridan,
The Rivals, 1775,
act II, scene i

1485 Silence is a friend who will never betray.
— Confucius,
Analects, ca. 500 B.C.,
book XVII, ch. 2

1486 There is a time for many words, and there is also a time for sleep.
— Homer, *The Odyssey,*
ca. 550 B.C.,
book XI, line 379

1487 He knew the precise psychological moment when to say nothing.
— Oscar Wilde,
The Picture of Dorian Gray,
1891, ch. 2

Simplicity

1488 The only image you should care about is the smile on the face of your customer as he enjoys your product or service, or on the face of your employee as he gets his share of the profits.
— Robert Townsend,
Further Up the Organization, 1984,
"Corporate Image"

1489 If you can't explain what you're doing in simple English, you are probably doing something wrong.
— Alfred Kahn,
Time, May 8, 1978

1490 Every simplification is an over-simplification.
— Alfred North Whitehead,
Adventures of Ideas,
1933, part III, ch. 15

1491 It is not at all simple to understand the simple.
— Eric Hoffer,
The Passionate State of Mind, 1954, no. 230

1492 One man's 'simple' is another man's 'huh?'
— David Stone,
Omni, May, 1979

1493 Nothing is so simple it cannot be misunderstood.
— Freeman Teague, Jr.,
Omni, May, 1979

Solutions

1494 What we see depends mainly on what we look for.
— John Lubbock, quoted by Peter Potter, *All About Success,* 1988, "Attitude"

1495 The first step to finding something is knowing where to look.
— Robert Half,
Robert Half on Hiring,
1985, ch. 3

1496 The precise statement of any problem is the most important step in its solution.
— Edwin C. Bliss,
Doing It Now,
1986, "Step 2: Develop a Game Plan"

1497 Never ever ever go to see the boss about a problem without bringing along a proposed solution. Better yet, three solutions.
— Walter Kiechel III,
Business Week,
Sept. 17, 1984

1498 You can have everything in life you want if you will just help enough other people get what they want.
— Zig Ziglar,
Top Performance,
1982, foreword

1499 In complicated situations, efforts to improve things often tend to make them worse, sometimes much worse, on occasion calamitous.
— Jay W. Forrester,
New York Times, June 4, 1971

1500 The more you use, the more you need to solve the problem.
— Sanford D. Garelik,
New York Times, March 23, 1971

1501 For every human problem, there is a neat, plain solution — and it is always wrong.
— H.L. Mencken, quoted in *Washingtonian,* Nov., 1978

1502 In a complex social system, the obvious, common-sense solution to a problem will turn out to be wrong most of the time.
— Jay W. Forrester,
New York Times,
Oct. 16, 1971

1503 Under certain circumstances, profanity pro-

vides a relief denied even to prayer.
— Mark Twain, quoted by Robert Byrne, *The 637 Best Things Anybody Ever Said,* 1982, no. 20

Statistics and Math

1504 *Acalculia, n.* the inability to work with numbers; a mental block against arithmetic.
— Josefa Heifetz Byrne, *Mrs. Byrne's Dictionary,* 1974

1505 The theory of probabilities is at bottom nothing but common sense reduced to calculus.
— Pierre Simon de Laplace, *Oeuvres,* volume VII, "Théorie Analytique des Probabilités," 1812, introduction

1506 Multiplication is vexation,
Division is as bad;
The rule of three doth puzzle me,
And practice drives me mad.
— Anonymous, ca. 1570

1507 Mathematics, rightly viewed, possesses not only truth, but supreme beauty — a beauty cold and austere, like that of sculpture.
— Bertrand Russell, *Mysticism and Logic,* 1918, ch. 4

1508 I have hardly ever known a mathematician who was capable of reasoning.
— Plato, *The Republic,* ca. 370 B.C., book VII, section 531

1509 Investors *want* to believe. Always looking for a better way, a chance to gain an advantage in the market, they are particularly susceptible to arguments that use statistics.
— Mark A. Johnson, *The Random Walk and Beyond,* 1988, ch. 3

1510 Statistics are mendacious truths.
— Lionel Strachey, quoted by Robert W. Kent, *Money Talks,* 1985, "Control"

1511 Most statistical research goes wrong or becomes biased right at the beginning, in the way it is set up. It may set us up, too.
— Mark A. Johnson, *The Random Walk and Beyond,* 1988, ch. 3

1512 Of those who quote statistics in conversation, 87 percent make up their numbers, 93 percent of the time.
— Michael C. Thomsett, *A Treasury of Business Quotations,* 1990, page 139

1513 There are two kinds of statistics, the kind you look up and the kind you make up.
— Rex Stout,
Death of a Doxy, 1966

Strength

1514 A thick skin is a gift from God.
— Konrad Adenauer, quoted by Roger von Oech,
A Kick in the Seat of the Pants, 1986,
"The Warrior"

1515 The gods are on the side of the stronger.
— Cornelius Tacitus,
The Histories,
ca. A.D. 95,
book IV, ch. 17

1516 You can only overcome your sensitivity to rejection by being rejected. As an entrepreneur your skin will get thick in a hurry.
— James R. Cook,
The Start-Up Entrepreneur,
1986, ch. 6

1517 Seek not out the things that are too hard for thee, neither search the things that are above thy strength.
— Bible: Apocrypha,
Ecclesiasticus 3:21

1518 The strong man in the world is he who stands most alone.
— Henrik Ibsen, *An Enemy of the People,* 1882, V

1519 Cast me not off in the time of old age; forsake me not when my strength faileth.
— Bible, Psalm 71:9

1520 The strongest is never strong enough to be always the master, unless he transforms strength into right, and obedience into duty.
— Jean-Jacques Rousseau,
The Social Contract,
1762, book I, ch. 3

1521 If a house be divided against itself, that house cannot stand.
— Bible, Mark 3:25

1522 It is the business of the very few to be independent; it is a privilege of the strong.
— Friedrich Nietzsche,
Beyond Good and Evil,
1886, no. 29

1523 Soft countries give birth to soft men.
— Herodotus, *The History,*
ca. 450 B.C., book IX, ch. 122

Success

1524 What is known as success assumes nearly as many

aliases as there are those who
seek it.
> —Stephen Birmingham,
> *Holiday,* March, 1961

1525 Each success only buys
an admission ticket to
a more difficult problem.
> —Henry A. Kissinger,
> *Wilson Library Bulletin,*
> March, 1979

1526 I know that unremit-
ting attention to business is
the price of success, but I don't
know what success is.
> —Charles Dudley Warner,
> *Backlog Studies,* 1873

1527 The need for challenge,
the need to burst through the
constrictions of tasks and situations already seen and
mastered, can affect anyone,
even those enjoying the greatest
gains from success.
> —Judith M. Bardwick,
> *The Plateauing Trap,*
> 1988, ch. 5

1528 Who never climbed
high never fell low.
> —Thomas Fuller,
> *Gnomologia,* 1732, no. 5713

1529 Success in life comes
not from holding a good hand,
but in playing a poor hand
well.
> —Denis Waitley and Remi
> L. Witt, *The Joy of
> Working,* 1985, "Day 9,
> Self-Expectation"

1530 To succeed in the
world, we do everything we can
to appear successful.
> —François, Duc de la
> Rochefoucauld, *Reflections;
> or, Sentences and Moral
> Maxims,* 1665, maxim 56

1531 Success is the reward
of anyone who looks for
trouble.
> —Walter Winchell, quoted
> by Peter Potter, *All About
> Success,* 1988, "Boldness"

1532 Success, a sort of
suicide,
Is ruin'd by success.
> —Edward Young,
> *Resignation,* 1762

1533 Even when people are
more successful than they had
imagined, nothing is ever
achieved without giving
something up.
> —Judith M. Bardwick,
> *The Plateauing Trap,*
> 1988, ch. 6

1534 For most entre-
preneurs, the process is its own
reward.
> —Deaver Brown,
> *The Entrepreneur's
> Guide,* 1980, ch. 1

1535 Success is not so much
achievement as achieving.
Refuse to join the cautious

crowd that plays not to lose; play to win.

—David J. Mahoney, quoted by Peter Potter, *All About Success,* 1988, "Secrets to Success"

1536 Success is a process, a quality of mind and way of being, an outgoing affirmation of life.

—Alex Noble, *Christian Science Monitor,* March 6, 1979

1537 Success doesn't mean the absence of failures; it means the attainment of ultimate objectives. It means winning the war, not every battle.

—Edwin C. Bliss, *Doing It Now,* 1986, "Step 3: Overcome Fear of Failure"

1538 Success . . . is much more difficult to deal with than failure, because only you will know how you are handling it.

—Harold Geneen with Alvin Moscow, *Managing,* 1984, ch. 8

1539 You have reached the pinnacle of success as soon as you become uninterested in money, compliments, or publicity.

—O.A. Battista, quoted by Peter Potter, *All About Success,* 1988, "Fame"

1540 Share your vision of success with your employees. It's something they can win if they put out the effort. They'll get excited about success when they know you're excited.

—Nicholas V. Iuppa, *Management by Guilt,* 1985, part 2

1541 At some time in the life cycle of virtually every organization, its ability to succeed in spite of itself runs out.

—Richard H. Brien, *The Educational Record,* 1970

1542 Those who tell you it's tough at the top have never been at the bottom.

—Joe Harvey, quoted by Peter Potter, *All About Success,* 1988, "Riches"

1543 If at first you don't succeed, you are running about average.

—M.H. Alderson, *Reader's Digest,* Feb., 1976

Tact

1544 *Charientism, n.* a gracefully veiled insult.

—Josefa Heifetz Byrne, *Mrs. Byrne's Dictionary,* 1974

1545 Tact is after all a kind of mind-reading.
—Sarah Orne Jewett,
The Country of the Pointed Firs, 1896, ch. 10

1546 Tact is the art of making a point without making an enemy.
—Howard W. Newton, quoted by Peter Potter, *All About Success,* 1988, "Tact"

1547 Never thank anybody for anything, except for a drink of water in the desert—and then make it brief.
—Gene Fowler, *New York Mirror,* April 9, 1954

1548 In the battle of existence, talent is the punch; tact is the clever footwork.
—Wilson Mizner, *Reader's Digest,* Feb., 1967

1549 Some people mistake weakness for tact. If they are silent when they ought to speak and so feign an agreement they do not feel, they call it being tactful. Cowardice would be a much better name.
—Frank Medlicott, *Reader's Digest,* July, 1958

1550 It's terribly difficult to offend people and influence them at the same time.
—Zig Ziglar, *Secrets of Closing the Sale,* 1984, ch. 32

1551 A diplomat is a person who can tell you to go to hell in such a way that you actually look forward to the trip.
—Caskie Stinnett, quoted by Peter Potter, *All About Success,* 1988, "Tact"

1552 Diplomacy is the art of saying "Nice doggie!" till you can find a rock.
—Wynn Catlin, quoted by Peter Potter, *All About Success,* 1988, "Conflict"

1553 Has this fellow no feeling of his business, that he sings at grave-making?
—William Shakespeare, *Hamlet,* 1601, act V, scene i, line 71

Thought

1554 *Omphaloskepsis, n.* meditation while gazing at one's navel.
—Josefa Heifetz Byrne, *Mrs. Byrne's Dictionary,* 1974

1555 What is the hardest talk in the world? To think.
— Ralph Waldo Emerson,
Essays: First Series,
1841, "Intellect"

1556 An attack upon systematic thought is treason to civilization.
— Alfred North Whitehead,
Adventures of Ideas,
1933, part II, ch. 10

1557 No truth so sublime but it may be trivial tomorrow in the light of new thoughts. People wish to be settled; only as far as they are unsettled is there any hope for them.
— Ralph Waldo Emerson,
Essays: First Series,
1841, "Circles"

1558 The last taboo of mankind, avoiding forbidden and dangerous thoughts, must be removed. There are no illegitimate thoughts.
— Theodor Reik,
The Need to Be Loved,
1963, part I, no. 6

1559 It is a far, far better thing to have a firm anchor in nonsense than to put out on the troubled seas of thought.
— John Kenneth Galbraith,
The Affluent Society,
1958, ch. 11

1560 Man is but a reed, the most feeble thing in nature; but he is a thinking reed.
— Blaise Pascal,
Pensées, 1670, no. 200

1561 The mind of man is like a clock that is always running down and requires to be as constantly wound up.
— William Hazlitt,
Sketches and Essays, 1839

1562 Whatever a man does he must do first in his mind.
— Albert Szent-Györgyi,
Saturday Review,
July 7, 1962

1563 Our life is what our thoughts make it.
— Marcus Aurelius
Antoninus, *Meditations,*
2nd century A.D.,
book IV, no. 3

1564 A great many people think they are thinking when they are merely rearranging their prejudices.
— William James,
Kansas City Times,
July 30, 1977

1565 A man is not idle because he is absorbed in thought. There is a visible labor and there is an invisible labor.
— Victor Hugo,
Les Misérables, 1862,
"Cosette," book VII, ch. 8

1566 The consistent thinker, the consistently moral man, is either a walking mummy or else, if he has not succeeded in stifling all his vitality, a fanatical monomaniac.
— Aldous Huxley,
Do What You Will, 1929

1567 A chief event of life is the day in which we have encountered a mind that startled us.
— Ralph Waldo Emerson,
Essays: Second Series,
1844, "Character"

1568 Practice and thought might gradually forge many an art.
— Virgil, *Georgics I,*
ca. 30 B.C., line 133

1569 Every thought is an exception to the general rule that people do not think.
— Paul Valéry,
Mauvaises Pensées et
Autres, 1941

1570 The habit most worth cultivating is that of thinking clearly even though inspired.
— Thomas H. Uzzell,
quoted by Robert W. Kent,
Money Talks, 1985,
"Communications"

1571 The worlds of thought and action overlap. What you

think has a way of becoming true.
— Roger von Oech,
A Whack on the Side of
the Head, 1983, ch. 10

1572 Beware when the great God lets loose a thinker on this planet. Then all things are at risk.
— Ralph Waldo Emerson,
Essays: First Series,
1841, "Circles"

1573 No one can be a great thinker who does not recognize that as a thinker it is his first duty to follow his intellect to whatever conclusions it may lead.
— John Stuart Mill,
On Liberty, 1859, ch. 2

1574 I am a fellow citizen of all men who think. Truth; that is my country.
— Alphonse de Lamartine,
Marseillaise de
la Paix, 1841

1575 Absence of thought is indeed a powerful factor in human affairs — statistically speaking the most powerful.
— Hannah Arendt,
New Yorker,
Nov. 28, 1977

1576 Something happens to a man when he puts on a

necktie. It cuts off all the oxygen to his brain.
— A.J. Carothers,
The Secret of My Success, 1987

1577 In this world second thoughts, it seems, are best.
— Euripides,
Hippolytus,
428 B.C., line 435

Time

1578 *Against time* or *against the clock, ad. phr.* 1. as a test of speed or time; in order to beat a speed record or time limit. 2. as fast as possible; so as to do or finish something before a certain time. 3. so as to cause delay by using up time.
— Maxine Tull Boatner,
J. Edward Gates, and
Adam Makkai, *A Dictionary of American Idioms,* 1987

1579 All life is a concatenation of ephemeralities.
— Alfred Kahn,
Barron's, Feb. 19, 1979

1580 Remember, that time is money.
— Benjamin Franklin,
Advice to a Young Tradesman, 1748

1581 Time cancels young pain.
— Euripides, *Alcestis,*
438 B.C., line 1085

1582 Time wounds all heels.
— Jane Ace,
Village Voice,
Dec. 26, 1977

1583 Time eases all things.
— Sophocles, *Oedipus Rex,*
ca. 430 B.C., line 1515

1584 Time carries away all things, even our wits.
— Virgil, *Eclogue IX,*
ca. 25 B.C., line 51

1585 Work expands to fill the time available for its completion.
— C. Northcote Parkinson,
Economist, Nov. 19, 1955

1586 Seldom is a matter of such a crisis nature that it justifies the interruption of a manager at work.
— Ronald Brown,
The Practical Manager's Guide to Excellence in Management, 1979, ch. 6

1587 As a carrier of your organization's vision, you have an important job in remembering, rehearsing, and helping others to remember the main event. This would be easier to do if there were fewer interruptions. Fragmentation characterizes the day.
— Priscilla Elfrey,
The Hidden Agenda,
1982, ch. 3

1588 Most people waste time making too many decisions. They make the same decisions over and over again because they can't retrieve earlier decision-making data.
— Philip Marvin,
Developing Decisions for Action, 1971, ch. 8

1589 You cannot fight against the future. Time is on our side.
— William E. Gladstone, speech, House of Commons, April 27, 1866

1590 Punctuality is a virtue that all men reverence in theory, but comparatively few carry into practice. Nothing inspires confidence in a business man sooner than this quality, nor is there any habit which is more disadvantageous than that of always being behind time.
— The Universal Self-Instructor, 1883, "Business Habits"

1591 Better three hours too soon than a minute too late.
— William Shakespeare, *The Merry Wives of Windsor,* 1601, act II, scene ii, line 332

1592 Half the time when men think they are talking business, they are wasting time.
— Edgar Watson Howe, quoted by Robert W. Kent, *Money Talks,* 1985, "Communications"

1593 Since the early bird catches the worm, it's a good idea to begin your day as soon as you can — unless, of course, you happen to be a worm.
— Edwin C. Bliss, *Doing It Now,* 1986, "Step 12: Learn to Deal with the Top Forty Cop-Outs"

1594 I wasted time, and now doth time waste me;
For now hath time made me his numbering clock;
My thoughts are minutes.
— William Shakespeare, *Richard II,* 1595, act V, scene v, line 49

1595 Time is flying, never to return.
— Virgil, *Georgics III,* ca. 30 B.C., line 284

1596 Lost time is never found again.
— Benjamin Franklin, *Poor Richard's Almanac,* Jan., 1748

1597 Next week there can't be any crisis. My schedule is already full.
— Henry A. Kissinger, *New York Times,* Oct. 28, 1973

Trust

1598 Silence is the best tactic for him who distrusts himself.
— François, Duc de la Rochefoucauld, *Reflections; or, Sentences and Moral Maxims,* 1665, maxim 79

1599 Let every eye negotiate for itself,
And trust no agent.
— William Shakespeare, *Much Ado About Nothing,* 1600, act II, scene i, line 187

1600 A man who trusts nobody is apt to be the kind of man nobody trusts.
— Harold Macmillan, *New York Herald Tribune,* Dec. 17, 1963

1601 Put not your trust in princes.
— Bible, Psalm 146:3

1602 A man who never trusts himself never trusts anyone.
— Paul de Gondi, *Memoirs,* 1665, book II

1603 I am very careful about bringing people into my confidence. I want to see the color of their eyes.
— E. Gerald Corrigan, *New York Times,* Dec. 30, 1984

1604 Men trust their ears less than their eyes.
— Herodotus, *The History,* ca. 450 B.C., book I, ch. 8

1605 Honor opens many doors and trust favorably influences the outcome of all your dealings.
— James R. Cook, *The Start-Up Entrepreneur,* 1986, ch. 4

1606 Show me a man who cannot bother to do little things and I'll show you a man who cannot be trusted to big things.
— Lawrence D. Bell, quoted by Peter Potter, *All About Success,* 1988, "Anything Worth Doing"

1607 Trust not him with your secrets, who, when left alone in your room, turns over your papers.
— Johann Kaspar Lavater, *Aphorisms on Man,* 1788, no. 449

Truth

1608 *Apodictic, adj.* clearly and undeniably true.
— Josefa Heifetz Byrne, *Mrs. Byrne's Dictionary,* 1974

1609 Let us begin by committing ourselves to the truth — to see it as it is, and tell it like

it is — to find the truth, to speak the truth, and to live the truth.
— Richard M. Nixon, nomination acceptance speech, 1968

1610 Better incur the trouble of testing and exploding a thousand fallacies than by rejecting, stifle a single beneficent Truth.
— Horace Greeley, *New York Tribune,* 1845

1611 The essential thing is not to find truth but to investigate and search for it.
— Max Nordau, *Paradoxes,* 1885, preface

1612 A thing is not proved because no one has ever questioned it ... Skepticism is the first step toward truth.
— Denis Diderot, *Pensées philosophiques,* 1746, book XXI

1613 There are two kinds of truth, small truth and great truth. You can recognize a small truth because its opposite is a falsehood. The opposite of a great truth is another truth.
— Niels Bohr, quoted by Roger von Oech, *A Whack on the Side of the Head,* 1983, "Breaktime"

1614 The truth is rarely pure, and never simple.
— Oscar Wilde, *The Importance of Being Earnest,* 1895, act I

1615 To know the truth partially is to distort the Universe.
— Alfred North Whitehead, *Adventures of Ideas,* 1933, part IV, ch. 16

1616 To love truth is the principal part of human perfection in this world, and the seed-plot of all other virtues.
— John Locke, letter, Oct. 29, 1703

1617 As one retiring chief executive said to his successor, "Yesterday was the last day you heard the truth from your subordinates."
— Robert W. McMurry, *Harvard Business Review,* 1965

1618 Truth fears nothing but concealment.
— The Universal Self-Instructor, 1983, "Legal Maxims"

1619 The truth is often unpopular and the contest between agreeable fancy and disagreeable fact is unequal. For, in the venacular, we Americans are suckers for good news.
— Adlai E. Stevenson, *New York Times,* June 9, 1958

1620 How dreadful knowledge of the truth can be when there's no help in truth.
— Sophocles, *Oedipus Rex,* ca. 430 B.C., line 316

1621 As scarce as truth is, the supply has always been in excess of the demand.
— Henry Wheeler Shaw,
Rocky Mountain News,
June 5, 1980

1622 Truth is all around you; what matters is where you put your focus.
— Roger von Oech,
A Whack on the Side of the Head, 1983, ch. 1

1623 No man thoroughly understands a truth until he has contended against it.
— Ralph Waldo Emerson,
Essays: First Series,
1841, "Compensation"

1624 Truth has a way of shifting under pressure.
— Curtis Bok,
Saturday Review,
Feb. 13, 1954

1625 If anyone in a discussion with us is not concerned with adjusting himself to truth, if he has no wish to find the truth, he is intellectually a barbarian.
— José Ortega y Gasset,
The Revolt of the Masses, 1930, ch. 8

1626 The first reaction to truth is hatred.
— Tertullian,
Apologeticus,
ca. 197, no. 7

1627 Experience and thought — or empirical knowledge and speculation — under the direction of reason, lead to the attainment of truth.
— Ernst Heinrich Haeckel,
The Wonders of Life,
1905, ch. 1

1628 Truth hath a quiet breast.
— William Shakespeare,
Richard II, 1595,
act I, scene iii, line 96

1629 Truth is on the march; nothing can stop it now.
— Émile Zola,
Le Figaro,
Nov. 25, 1897

1630 Speak boldly, and speak truly,
Shame the devil.
— John Fletcher,
Wit Without Money,
1614, act IV

1631 Each generation of critics does nothing but take the opposite of the truths accepted by their predecessors.
— Marcel Proust,
Remembrance of Things Past,
1913–1926, volume III,
"The Guermantes Way"

1632 Nobody speaks the truth when there's something they must have.
— Elizabeth Bowan,
The House in Paris,
1935, part I, ch. 5

1633 I speak truth not so much as I would, but as much as I dare, and I dare a little more as I grow older.
— Michel Eyquem de Montaigne, *Essays,* 1580–1595, book III, ch. 1

1634 It takes two to speak the truth — one to speak and another to hear.
— Henry David Thoreau, *A Week on the Concord and Merrimack Rivers,* 1849, "Wednesday"

1635 'The true,' to put it briefly, is only the expedient in the way of our thinking, just as 'the right' is only the expedient in the way of our behaving.
— William James, *Pragmatism,* 1907, lecture 6

1636 Keep in mind that 99.44 percent of the truth is about as big a dose as anyone can handle. The other .56 percent is lethal. Resist the temptation to disclose the deadly part of the message.
— Nicholas V. Iuppa, *Management by Guilt,* 1985, part 2

1637 Truth is great and its effectiveness endures.
— Ptahhotep, *The Maxims of Ptahhotep,* ca. 2350 B.C., maxim no. 5

1638 Truth in advertising, and in business, is neither likely nor entirely possible.
— Neal W. O'Connor, quoted by Robert W. Kent, *Money Talks,* 1985, "Marketing"

1639 We are born to inquire into truth; it belongs to a greater power to possess it.
— Michel Eyquem de Montaigne, *Essays,* 1580–1595, book III, ch. 8

1640 Marvelous Truth, comfort us at every turn, in every guise.
— Denise Lavertov, *Matins,* 1962, VII

1641 God offers to every mind a choice between truth and repose. Take which you please — you can never have both.
— Ralph Waldo Emerson, *Essays: First Series,* 1841, "Intellect"

1642 No generalization is wholly true, not even this one.
— Oliver Wendell Holmes, Jr. (attributed)

1643 There was things which he stretched, but mainly he told the truth.
— Mark Twain, *The Adventures of Huckleberry Finn,* 1884, ch. 1

1644 You should never have your best trousers on when you turn out to fight for freedom and truth.

> — Henrik Ibsen,
> *An Enemy of the People,*
> 1882, act V

Understanding

1645 *Put across, v.* 1. to explain clearly; make yourself understood; communicate.
2. *informal* to get (something) done successfully; bring to success; make real.

> — Maxine Tull Boatner,
> J. Edward Gates, and Adam
> Makkai, *A Dictionary of
> American Idioms,* 1987

1646 You cannot conceive the many without the one.

> — Plato, *Parmenides,*
> ca. 350 B.C., section 166

1647 Be not curious in unnecessary matters: for more things are showed onto thee than men understand.

> — Bible: Apocrypha,
> Ecclesiasticus 3:23

1648 Some people will never learn anything, for this reason, because they understand everything too soon.

> — Alexander Pope, quoted
> by Peter Potter, *All About
> Success,* 1988, "Priorities"

1649 There is a vast difference between understanding something well enough to buy it as opposed to understanding it well enough to sell it.

> — Zig Ziglar,
> *Secrets of Closing
> the Sale,* 1984, ch. 21

1650 To be surprised, to wonder, is to begin to understand. This is the sport, the luxury, special to the intellectual man.

> — José Ortega y Gasset,
> *The Revolt of the Masses,*
> 1930, ch. 1

1651 If you are sure you understand everything that is going on, you are hopelessly confused.

> — Walter Mondale,
> *Poughkeepsie Journal,*
> March 26, 1978

1652 The more I understand myself, the more effectively I can work with others.

> — Zig Ziglar,
> *Top Performance,*
> 1982, ch. 10

1653 It is difficult to get a man to understand something when his salary depends upon his not understanding it.

> — Upton Sinclair, quoted
> by Robert W. Kent,
> *Money Talks,* 1985,
> "Communications"

Virtue and Vice

1654 Virtue is not always amiable.
—John Adams, diary,
Feb. 9, 1779

1655 Few men have virtue to withstand the highest bidder.
—George Washington,
letter, Aug. 17, 1779

1656 A man who wants to act virtuously in every way necessarily comes to grief among so many who are not virtuous.
—Niccolò Machiavelli,
The Prince,
1513, ch. 5

1657 If you give me six sentences written by the most innocent of men, I will find something in them with which to hang him.
—Armand Jean du Plessis,
Mirame, ca. 1625

1658 The superior man thinks of virtue; the small man thinks of comfort.
—Confucius,
Analects,
ca. 500 B.C., book II

1659 There is never an instant's truce between virtue and vice. Goodness is the only investment that never fails.
—Henry David Thoreau,
Walden, 1854,
11, "Higher Laws"

1660 Our virtues are most often but our vices disguised.
—François, Duc de la
Rochefoucauld, *Reflections; or,*
Sentences and Moral Maxims,
1665, maxim 1

1661 There is no vice so simple but assumes
Some mark of virtue on his outward parts.
—William Shakespeare,
The Merchant of Venice,
1596, act III,
scene ii, line 81

1662 Though ambition in itself is a vice, yet it is often the parent of virtues.
—Quintilian,
Institutio Oratoria,
1st century A.D., book I

1663 Moderation in temper is always a virtue, but moderation in principle is always a vice.
—Thomas Paine,
The Rights of Man, 1792

1664 To be possessed of good mental power is not sufficient; the principal matter is to apply them well. The greatest minds are capable of the greatest vices as well as of the greatest virtues.
—René Descartes,
Discourse on the Method,
1637, part I

1665 I prefer an accommodating vice to an obstinate virtue.
—Molière, *Amphitryon,*
1666, act I, scene iv

Wealth

1666 *Aphnology, n.* the science of wealth.
—Josefa Heifetz Byrne,
Mrs. Byrne's Dictionary, 1974

1667 Broker: the end-result of turning a large fortune into a small one.
—Kurt Brouwer,
Unusual Investment Definitions, 1987

1668 Riches have wings, and grandeur is a dream.
—William Cowper,
The Task, 1785,
book III, "The Garden,"
line 265

1669 Nothing could discredit capitalism more than a decision by the Russians to try it.
—Jack Tanner,
Challenger,
March/April, 1976

1670 He that trusteth in his riches shall fall: but the righteous shall flourish as a branch.
—Bible, Proverbs 11:28

1671 Riches cover a multitude of woes.
—Menander, *Fragment 90,*
3rd century B.C.

1672 I've never been poor, only broke. Being poor is a frame of mind. Being broke is only a temporary situation.
—Mike Todd,
Newsweek,
March 31, 1958

1673 We all live in a state of ambitious poverty.
—Juvenal, *Satires,*
ca. A.D. 110,
book III, line 182

1674 When you earn it and spend it you do know the difference between three dollars and a million dollars, but when you say it and vote it, it all sounds the same.
—Gertrude Stein,
Saturday Evening Post,
June 13, 1936

1675 To turn $100 into $110 is work. To turn $100 million into $110 million is inevitable.
—Edgar Bronfman,
Newsweek,
Dec. 2, 1985

1676 To suppose, as we all suppose, that we could be rich and not behave as the rich behave, is like supposing that we could drink all day and keep absolutely sober.

—Logan Pearsall Smith,
Afterthoughts, 1931,
ch. 4, "In the World"

1677 If all the rich men in the world divided up their money amongst themselves, there wouldn't be enough to go round.

—Christina Stead, quoted by Robert W. Kent,
Money Talks, 1985,
"Macroeconomics"

1678 The greater the wealth, the thicker will be the dirt. This indubitably describes a tendency of our time.

—John Kenneth Galbraith,
The Affluent Society,
1958, ch. 17

1679 A mere madness, to live like a wretch and die rich.

—Robert Burton, quoted by Robert W. Kent,
Money Talks,
1985, "Business Is and Business As"

1680 He who wishes to be rich in a day will be hanged in a year.

—Leonardo da Vinci,
Notebooks, ca. 1500

1681 The man who dies rich dies disgraced.

—Andrew Carnegie,
North American Review,
June, 1889

1682 If the rich could hire other people to die for them, the poor could make a wonderful living.

—Yiddish proverb

Wisdom

1683 Wisdom is the supreme part of happiness.

—Sophocles,
Antigone,
ca. 440 B.C., line 1347

1684 Nine-tenths of wisdom is being wise in time.

—Theodore Roosevelt,
speech, June 14, 1917

1685 A man only becomes wise when he begins to calculate the approximate depth of his ignorance.

—Gian Carlo Menotti,
New York Times,
April 14, 1974

1686 Knowledge shrinks as wisdom grows.

—Alfred North Whitehead,
*Aims of Education
and Other Essays,*
1929, ch. 3

1687 Wisdom consists of the anticipation of consequences.

—Norman Cousins,
Saturday Review,
April 15, 1978

1688 The art of being wise is the art of knowing what to overlook.
— William James, *The Principles of Psychology,* 1890, ch. 22

1689 A wise man sees as much as he ought, not as much as he can.
— Michel Eyquem de Montaigne, quoted by Peter Potter, *All About Success,* 1988, "Discretion"

1690 You understand human nature when you are never surprised by anything it does.
— Vernon Howard, quoted by Peter Potter, *All About Success,* 1988, "Wisdom"

1691 The price of wisdom is above rubies.
— Bible, Job 28:18

1692 Life is a festival only to the wise.
— Ralph Waldo Emerson, *Essays: First Series,* 1841, "Heroism"

1693 With the ancient is wisdom; and in length of days understanding.
— Bible, Job 12:12

1694 It may almost be a question whether such wisdom as many of us have in our mature years has not come from the dying out of the power of temptation, rather than as the result of thought and resolution.
— Anthony Trollope, *The Small House at Allington,* 1864, ch. 14

1695 Great men are not always wise.
— Bible, Job 32:9

1696 Wisdom is the principal thing; therefore get wisdom: and with all thy getting get understanding.
— Bible, Proverbs 4:7

1697 Young men's minds are light as air, but when an old man comes he looks before and after, deeming that which shall be fairest upon both sides.
— Homer, *The Iliad,* ca. 550 B.C., book III, line 108

1698 Be not overwise in doing thy business.
— Bible: Apocrypha, Ecclesiasticus 10:26

1699 The wise man is satisfied with nothing.
— William Godwin, *An Inquiry Concerning Political Justice, and Its Influence on General Virtue and Happiness,* 1793, book IV, ch. 1

Words

1700 *Altiloquence, n.* pompous speech.
—Josefa Heifetz Byrne,
Mrs. Byrne's Dictionary, 1974

1701 Nobody has a right to speak more clearly than he thinks.
—Alfred North Whitehead,
Washingtonian, Nov., 1979

1702 You just never learn anything when you're talking.
—Jeffrey G. Allen,
Surviving Corporate Downsizing, 1988, ch. 1

1703 Experience shows over and over again that there is nothing which men have less power over than the tongue.
—Baruch Spinoza,
Ethics, 1677,
part III, proposition 2

1704 Remember, every time you open your mouth to talk, your mind walks out and parades up and down the words.
—Edwin H. Stuart, quoted by Peter Potter,
All About Success,
1988, "Talk"

1705 Talkers are no good doers.
—William Shakespeare,
Richard III, 1593,
act I, scene iii, line 351

1706 He's a wonderful talker, who has the art of telling you nothing in a great harangue.
—Molière,
Le Misanthrope,
1666, act II, scene v

1707 How long a time lies in one little word!
—William Shakespeare,
Richard II,
1595, act I,
scene iii, line 213

1708 If you tell every step, you will make a long journey of it.
—Thomas Fuller,
Gnomologia,
1732, no. 2793

1709 I have never yet been used to holding long conversations with people, and am ashamed to begin questioning one who is so much older than myself.
—Homer, *The Odyssey,*
ca. 550 B.C.,
book III, line 24

1710 Beware of the man who will not engage in idle conversation; he is planning to steal your walking stick or water your stock.
—William Emerson,
Newsweek,
Oct. 29, 1973

1711 I understand a fury in
your words,
But not the words.
> —William Shakespeare,
> *Othello,* 1605, act IV,
> scene ii, line 31

1712 Words are weapons,
and it is dangerous in speculation, as in politics, to borrow
them from our enemies.
> —George Santayana,
> *Obiter Scripta,* 1936

1713 How often misused
words generate misleading
thoughts.
> —Herbert Spencer,
> *Principles of Ethics,*
> 1892–1893, book I, ch. 8

1714 Ill deeds are doubled
with an evil word.
> —William Shakespeare,
> *The Comedy of Errors,* 1592,
> act III, scene ii, line 20

1715 It is better that words
shall have no interpretation
than an absurd one.
> —The Universal Self-
> Instructor, 1883,
> "Legal Maxims"

1716 Words pay no debts.
> —William Shakespeare,
> *Troilus and Cressida,* 1603,
> act III, scene ii, line 56

1717 My duty is to speak; I
have no wish to be an
accomplice.
> —Émile Zola, letter,
> Jan. 15, 1898

1718 Without knowing the
force of words, it is impossible
to know men.
> —Confucius, *Analects,*
> ca. 500 B.C.,
> book XX, ch. 3

1719 Human speech is like a
cracked kettle on which we tap
crude rhythms for bears to
dance to, while we long to make
music that will melt the stars.
> —Gustave Flaubert,
> *Madame Bovary,*
> 1857, part II, ch. 12

1720 Words are, of course,
the most powerful drug used by
mankind.
> —Rudyard Kipling,
> speech, Feb. 14, 1923

1721 Words are healers of
the sick tempered.
> —Aeschylus,
> *Prometheus Bound,*
> ca. 460 B.C., line 380

1722 A word fitly spoken is
like apples of gold in pictures of
silver.
> —Bible, Proverbs 25:11

1723 How forcible are right
words!
> —Bible, Job 6:25

1724 I'll speak in a
monstrous little voice.
> —William Shakespeare,
> *A Midsummer Night's Dream,*
> 1595, act I,
> scene ii, line 55

1725 Soft words are hard arguments.
— Thomas Fuller,
Gnomologia,
1732, no. 4203

1726 Good words are worth much, and cost little.
— George Herbert,
Jacula Prudentum,
1651, no. 155

1727 The words fell from his lips sweeter than honey.
— Homer, *The Iliad,*
ca. 550 B.C.,
book I, line 249

1728 Long words and complex sentences are intended to add importance to something unimportant.
— Jack Mabley,
Detroit Free Press,
Nov. 2, 1981

1729 Proper words in proper places make the true definition of style.
— Jonathan Swift,
letter,
Jan. 9, 1720

1730 Words are wise men's counters, they do but reckon with them, but they are the money of fools.
— Thomas Hobbes,
Leviathan, 1651,
part I, ch. 4

1731 Slang is a language that rolls up its sleeves, spits on its hands, and goes to work.
— Carl Sandburg,
New York Times,
Feb. 13, 1959

Work

1732 Routine is the god of every social system; it is the seventh heaven of business, the essential component in the success of every factory, the idea of every statesman.
— Alfred North Whitehead,
Adventures of Ideas,
1933, part I, ch. 6

1733 Farmer, laborer, clerk: That's a brief history of the United States.
— John Naisbitt,
Megatrends,
1984, ch. 1

1734 Only rarely can we get the best possible picture of a man in relation to the requirements of a job without his cooperation.
— Richard A. Fear,
The Evaluation Interview,
1973, ch. 1

1735 Word is the grand cure of all the maladies and miseries that ever beset mankind.
— Thomas Carlyle,
speech, April 2, 1886

1736 People don't choose their careers; they are engulfed by them.
— John Dos Passos,
New York Times,
Oct. 25, 1959

1737 Perpetual devotion to what a man calls his business, is only to be sustained by perpetual neglect of many other things.
— Robert Louis Stevenson,
Virginibus Puerisque, 1881,
III, "An Apology for Idlers"

1738 I like work; it fascinates me. I can sit and look at it for hours. I love to keep it by me: the idea of getting rid of it nearly breaks my heart.
— Jerome K. Jerome,
Three Men in a Boat,
1889, ch. 15

1739 Life without industry is guilt, industry without art is brutality.
— John Ruskin,
Lectures on Art,
1870, III, "The Relation of Art to Morals"

1740 Work is hard. Distractions are plentiful. And time is short.
— Adam Hochschild,
New York Times,
Feb. 5, 1985

1741 Life grants nothing to us mortals without hard work.
— Horace, *Satires,*
35 B.C., book I,
satire ix, line 59

1742 When you cease to make a contribution, you begin to die.
— Eleanor Roosevelt,
letter, Feb. 19, 1960

1743 There is as much dignity in tilling a field as in writing a poem.
— Booker T. Washington,
speech, Sept. 9, 1895

1744 The reason worry kills more people than work is that more people worry than work.
— Robert Frost, *Vogue,*
March 15, 1963

Author Index

A

Abailard, Pierre, *see* Abélard, Pierre
Abedi, Agha Hasan, 1125
Abel, Lionel, 901
Abélard, Pierre, 1366
Abrams, Mark, 1006
Aburdene, Patricia, 42, 113, 209, 476, 875, 937, 1129, 1328
Ace, Jane, 1582
Acheson, Dean, 1081
Acton, Lord, *see* Dalberg, John E.E.
Adams, Franklin P., 871
Adams, Henry Brooks, 706, 893, 1199
Adams, John, 1654
Addison, Joseph, 76, 834
Ade, George, 273
Adenauer, Konrad, 1514
Adler, Alfred, 1433
Adler, Fred, 192
Adler, Mortimer J., 817
Aeschylus, 496, 559, 775, 1220, 1721
Aesop, 9, 783, 1041, 1156, 1247, 1360
Afer, Publius Terentius, *see* Terence
Ahern, Tom, 355, 357
Alderson, M.H., 1543
Alito, Noelie, 1240
Allen, Agnes, 1287, 1297
Allen, Fred, 1060
Allen, Jeffrey G., 366, 515, 522, 1155, 1355, 1367, 1702
Allen, Woody, 306, 954
Amiel, Henri Frédéric, 933, 1033
Anderson, Marian, 1152
Anderson, Paul, 1295
Annenberg, Walter, 52
Anthony, William P., 11, 171
Antoninus, Marcus Aurelius, 350, 798, 801, 1150, 1211, 1563
Arbiter, Petronius, *see* Petronius, Gaius
Arendt, Hannah, 1575
Aristocles, *see* Plato
Aristophanes, 19, 212, 244, 289, 399, 534, 707, 804, 806
Aristotle, 72, 667, 767, 941

Arouet, François Marie, *see* Voltaire
Ascham, Roger, 1393
Ash, Mary Kay, 101
Athos, Anthony G., 978
Atkinson, Brooks, 167
Avebury, Baron, *see* Lubbock, John

B

Bacon, Francis, 418, 1224
Bagehot, Walter, 46
Baida, Peter, 1078
Baker, Ray Stannard, *see* Grayson, David
Baker, Russell, 774
Ball, George, 1024
Banning, Margaret Culkin, 581
Bardwick, Judith M., 361, 724, 729, 1451, 1453, 1527, 1533
Barker, J. Hopps, 440
Barth, John, 1333
Barton, Bruce, 485, 1456
Battista, O.A., 1539
Bear, John, 193, 199, 287, 526
Beaumarchais, Pierre de, 1054
Becker, Gordon, 1303
Beecher, Henry Ward, 235
Behn, Aphra, 1099
Bell, Lawrence D., 1606
Benchley, Robert, 233, 947
Bentley, Eric, 239
Bequai, August, 329
Berenson, Bernard, 346
Bernbach, William, 25
Berra, Yogi, 1149
Berst, Jesse, 569
Bevan, Aneurin, 184
Beveridge, W.I., 204
Bible, 40, 41, 50, 86, 90, 226, 245, 248, 261, 351, 423, 425, 490, 501, 503, 560, 605, 681, 690, 702, 708, 745, 748, 750, 752, 757, 761, 778, 915, 952, 1014, 1016, 1092, 1147, 1251, 1268, 1305, 1389, 1392, 1403, 1517,

161

Key Word Index

A

ability: business a. of the man, 21; merit and a., 1038; of man to elevate, 8; one's a. to perform, 13; ordinary a., 1124; to arrive at, 409; to impress, 96; to succeed, 1541
able: man, 1438; to think, 278
abound: in knowledge, 1262
absence: of failures, 1537; of thought, 1575
absent: are always wrong, 1075
absolutely: in our power, 1263
absorbed: in thought, 1565
abstraction: levels of a., 364
accept: people will a. your ideas, 4
acceptance: by flattery, 678; familiarity breeds a., 88; of. . .a change, 214
accepting: yourself, 1453
access: willing to allow a., 1412
accident: call it an a., 47
accidents: shackles a., 218
accommodating: vice, 1665
accomplice: hand an a. the goods, 1204; no wish to be an a., 1717
accomplish: by avoiding doing things you a., 36; having to a., 30; no harm in wanting to a., 30; who reflects too much will a. little, 33
accomplishments: credentials are not same as a., 29; give luster, 28
accountability: is demanded, 49; relinquish a., 433
accountants: are perpetually fighting, 1446; can be smarter, 989; write about anything, 1399
accusations: doubtful a., 925
achieve: never will you a. anything, 39; want to a., 724; you must a., 1259
achievement: creative a., 1250; despite the most enormous a., 35
achievements: ambiguity of one's highest a., 34; on their a., 523

achieving: success is. . .a., 1535
acquisition: chain letter, 1264; of [knowledge], 945
across: put a., 1645
act: Congress can't a., 182; very obnoxious a., 55; virtuously, 1656
acting: reason for not a., 1301
action: ancestor of every a., 64; any worthwhile a., 217; calls to a., 1369; course of a., 414; cowed by the name of a., 64; for every a., 181; ideas into a., 419; idiocy of human a., 61; in each a., we must look, 62; is best which procures, 66; is the proper fruit of knowledge, 54; knowledge must come through a., 71; man of a., 65; political a., 1020; power over a., 1262; rightness of a., 94; thought and a., 1571; truth in a., 908; your every a., 896
actions: in his a., be so ill, 60; noblest a., 1134; responsible for all our a., 57
activities: day-to-day a., 321; functional a., 252
activity: happiness is a., 767; leisure a., 1006; of money, 1113
acts: from the passions, 67; involuntary a., 57; voluntary a., 57
adequate: reason, 1301
adherence: automatic a., 474
adjustment: every new a., 1454
administration: between management and a., 165
admire: without desiring, 779
admission: ticket, 1525
ado: is about himself, 290
advance: of time, 1169
advancement: often depends, 94
advances: in science, 1351
advantage: gain an a., 1509; three-to-one a., 1346; to the other fellow, 352; to you, 798
adventure: capacity for one a., 1411
adversity: causes some men to break,

299; hidden in a., 708; in the face
of a., 315; men can bear a., 310
advertising: first law in a., 1470; is a
valuable economic factor, 1469: is
what you do, 1468; may be described, 1473; truth in a., 1638
advice: after injury, 84; as to a., be
wary, 383; is not disliked, 79;
receive with so much reluctance as
a., 76; start giving a., 77; the
smallest common coin, 74; to any
young person, 1170; to ask a., 679
advise: happy to a., others, 80
advisers: to rich men, 465
affairs: application...to a., 922; control a., 1274; human a., 1575; prosper, 1180
affected: to trade, 1131
affiliations: web of intricate a., 259
affirmation: from others, 1453; of life,
1536
affliction: forgetfulness of a., 1092
after: before and a., 1697
age: frittering away his a., 841; industrial a., 937; of substitutes, 239;
old a., 1519; or experience, 981;
pressure of a., 772; trouble with
our a., 722; uncertainties of one a.,
1285
agencies: autonomous a., 174
agent: trust no a., 1599
agree: how a. the kettle and the
earthen pot, 90; you a. with me, 93
agreeable: fancy, 1619
agreed: except they be a., 86
agreement: feign an a., 1549;
gentlemen's a., 92; keep to the a.,
1116
ailment: that afflicts people, 317
aims: heroic a., 244
air: castles in the a., 742; light as a.,
1697
aliases: many a., 1524
all: of the answers, 1368
alone: stands most a., 1518
aloofness: mediocrity requires a., 1050
alternatives: absence of a., 411
America: best-kept secrets in A., 113;
corporate A., 1463; if A. is to
move, 1311;
American: companies, 1402; people,
1034; secrets in A. business, 1253;
superstition, 655; way, 1340
Americans: are so enamored, 917;

are suckers for good news, 1619
ambiguity: in the world, 374; of one's
highest achievements, 34; take
refuge in a., 250; uncertainty and
imperfection, 978
ambition...is a vice, 1662
ambitious: more a., 989; poverty,
1673; very few people are a., 724
amiable: not always a., 1654
amount: of punishment, 865
anchor: in nonsense, 1559
ancient: with the a. is widom, 1693
anesthetic: that dulls the pain, 483
animal: be a good a., 602
animals: like other a., 1414
annihilation: neighbor to a., 309
annoyance: of a good example, 1165
annual: message in an a. report, 1401;
put in their a. reports, 1402; report
is a...public relations tool, 1400;
reports are the product, 1399
anonymous: and nonheroic, 1422
another: truth, 1613
answer: deserves an a., 1373; not the
a., 1370; promptly, 1179; which cannot be expressed, 1371
answers: all of the a., 1368; cynics
know the a., 649; easy a., 1374;
hastily contrived a., 1369; interesting a., 1375; right a., 1372;
right or wrong a., 414; they can
only give you a., 277
anticipation: of consequences, 1687
antidote: to fear, 932
antiseptic: environment, 1465
ants: live like a., 817
anybody: can win, 273; who gets
away with something, 923
anyone: can hold the helm, 990; who
does not feel...strong, 1026
anything: but profit, 1323; more I can
do, 1409; never take a., 118; so
remorseless, 1015; that happens
enough times, 1087
apathy: indifference and a., 550
appearance: of dinosaurs mating, 1266
appearances: satisfied with a., 1380
apples: of gold, 1722
application: to affairs, 922
appreciate: the strength, 267
approach: makes the a. work, 1381;
new a., 666; traditional a., 1244
approval: of others, 504
arbitrary: values, 1472

B

brakeman: progress needs the b., 1342

branch: flourish as a b., 1670

break: your word, 798

breast: quiet b., 1628

breeding: ill b., 332; man or woman's b., 293

brevity: is the soul of wit, 802

bridge: going to be a b., 530

brief: history, 1733; make it b., 1547; when I struggle to be b., 249

briefcases: fill the available b., 189

brilliance: without the capability, 888

broke: being b. only a temporary situation, 1672

brutal: voice, 19

brutality: industry without art is b., 1739

buck: pass the b., 428

buckets: empty b., 841

budget: balancing the b., 158; believe in the b., 157; control system (b.), 155; for the coming year, 154; is a statement of priorities, 149; is big enough, 394; luxuries your b. can afford, 148; should be a door, 153

budgeting: is a black art, 147

budgets: are good for, 150; ...are not taken seriously, 152

built-in: filters, 1184

bullets: will go right through them, 500

bum: you're a b., 819

bundle: of contradictions, 341

burden: another's, 1415; equally a b., 772

bureaucracy: argument...within the b., 164; defends the status quo, 172; is nothing more, 171; original thought in a b., 166; that does not like a poem, 188; the rule of no one, 176; well-articulated b., 187

bureaucrat: if Moses had been a b., 159; it's a poor b., 168; like a b. scorned, 160; makes a mistake, 169; perfect b., 167

bureaucratic: growth, 175; magicians, 147; regulations, 163; system, 173

bureaucrats: are the only people, 161; guidelines for b., 170; what b. used to do exclusively, 165

buried: in committees, 1065

burning: fast b., 1086

business: American b., 730, 1253; at-

tention to b., 1526; big b., 870; certainly needs managers, 966; confidence in a b. man, 1590; doing thy b., 1698; dreams, 1243; everybody's b., 759, 1326; fit for b., 426; haste in every b., 786; in b., 1325; in hand, 783; industry and b., 998; ...is a continual dealing, 1254; is like riding a bicycle, 1344; is many things, 1356; is never really good or bad, 112; is...war and sport, 268; language of b., 1314; legitimate b., 603; man calls his b., 1737; man of b., 731; never acquire a b., 949; no feeling of his b., 1553; nobody's b., 759; of life, 1338; of the very few, 1522; one tenth of us who are in b., 1357; pages, 238; plan, 192; precept, 1164; running a b., 1381; school formulas, 967; seventh heaven of b., 1732; strictly honest b., 790; success in b., 1123; successful b., 405; talking b., 1592; techniques of b., 153; truth in...b., 1638; world, 628, 1049

businessmen: commit a fraud, 1323

busy: man, 1309; person, 1310; trying to look b., 846

buy: anything you want, 329; don't b. a $10,000...sledgehammer, 199; never b. anything you can't lift, 193; people b. what they want, 197; people don't b., 194

buyer: needs a hundred eyes, 198

buying: we are constantly b., 195

byproducts: of goal setting, 727

C

cabals: are everywhere, 1161

calculate: begins to c., 1685

calculation: continual c., 1254

calculations: out of your c., 1261

calculus: common sense reduced to c., 1505

calf: lion and the c., 306

calm: and happy nature, 772; when the sea is c., 990

candidate: who hires the best, 511

candidates: job c., 96

canvas: blank c. of the businessman, 368

capabilities: inherent c., 982

Key Word Index

D

F

fails: never f., 1659; when all else f., 1297

failure: ask any f., 1035; benefits of f., 666; cannot be blamed for subordinates, 433; fear of f., 658; formula for f., 659; hopeless f., 21; is instructive, 663; [learn] much from f., 664; more difficult...than f., 1538; term for f., 624; to grow, 1337; to realize, 1197; wisdom through f., 662

failures: absence of f., 1537; deepest f., 34; haste brings f., 786

fair: exterior is a silent recommendation, 95

fairest: upon both sides, 1697

faith: articles of f., 674; comes in moments, 675; fantastic f., 676; means not wanting, 673; overwhelming f., 1456; that stands in authority, 677

faithful: mentally f. himself, 124

fall: prevent a f., 573

fallacies: exploding a thousand f., 1610

false: absolutely f., 130; ideas, 1176; idle and most f., 919; sense of security, 1440; state of security, 1442; to any man, 1012

falsehood: and truth, 1027; opposite is a f., 1613; some dear f., 676; violated by f., 1033

falsehoods: if there were no f., 1023

fame: preserve their f., 1177

familiarity: breeds acceptance, 88

fancy: agreeable f., 1619

fantasy: world, 1383

far: aiming at what's f., 735

farming: looks mighty easy, 1378

fast: as possible, 1578

fat: cats in the staff, 185

fatigue: of judging, 906

fault: cannot be found, 1360; confesss a f., 576; little f., 337

faults: find them without f., 711; greatest of all f., 607; if we had no f., 1449; molded out of f., 620; notice your f., 77; small f., 389

favor: do someone a f., 535

fear: always be in f., 1426; antidote to f., 932; loathing and the f., 1253; of [boredom], 142; of disgrace, 103; of meeting people, 1058; of responsibility, 1404; the birds of prey, 957; we f. it, 1049

feast: is made for laughter, 778

feathers: largest possible amount of f., 462

feedback: from...change, 217

feeling: never ignore a gut f., 422; transference of f., 1459

feet: are guided, 625

fellow: citizen, 1574; nice f., 700; other f., 352, 809; who is...far removed, 1203

festival: life is a f., 1692

few: and far between, 1038; men have virtue, 1655; men of f. words, 1477

fibers: multitude of f., 566

fickle: changeable and f., 1177

field: in the f., 1196; tilling a f., 1743

fields: change f., 1351

fight: against the future, 1589; for freedom and truth, 1644; good reason to f., 302; to the death, 288; fighting: their...image, 1446

filing: is concerned with the past, 1308

filters: built-in f., 1184

financial: matters, 1399; types, 1377

financier: is a pawnbroker, 1010

find: and develop...talent, 1387; out the shortcomings, 1061; reality, 1383; something in them, 1657; the truth, 1609; yourself doing, 1129

fingernails: hanging on by my f., 1352

fingerprints: personal as f., 581

fire: without light, 545

fired: you're f., 1452

firm: a proud Victorian word, 105; anchor in nonsense, 1559; responsiveness of a f., 260

first: duty, 1573; key to wisdom, 1366; law in advertising, 1470; reaction to truth, 1626; step, 1612

first-rate: people, 517

fish: only dead f. swim with the stream, 328; surrounded by f., 184

fit: for business, 426

fittest: will survive, 1160

flag: law is a f., 956

flame: bursting into f., 1086

flashes: draws the f., 1052

flatterer: can risk, 683

flatterers: guard oneself from f., 680

flattereth: with his lips, 681

flattery: acceptance by f., 678; love of f., 684; taken by f., 682; tout for f., 679

flexibility: destroys f., 1055

future: confidence in. . .f., 133; dealing with the f., 1254; faced the f., 1183; fight against the f., 1589; has to do with the f., 1308; predicting a family's f., 466; refugees of a f., 672; say something about the f., 671; that period of time, 1180; think about the f., 1233

G

gain: make g., 1330
gains: greatest g., 1527
gall: enough in thy ink, 1084
gallantry: to do with g., 333
game: chess g., 1267; managers in the g., 1206; risk/return g., 1432
games: play political g., 357
gathering: of important people, 1060
gaudy: cheap or g., 1353
general: rule, 1569; sense of optimism, 1376
generalization: no g. is wholly true, 1642
generation: of critics, 1631
genius: all over the world, 718; death of g., 392; everybody is born with g., 720; forgive everything except g., 719; has its limits, 721; [is] little more, 714; is one of the many forms, 716; is the ability, 715; no g., 1023; only an organizing g., 184; when a true g. appears, 717
gentleman: he was a g., 1319
geometric: growth, 1264; ratio, 1290
gift: from God, 1514; word better than a g., 1392
gifts: of a bad man, 403
give: to get, 1155
glory: desire for g., 1277; triumph without g., 1418
glue: moral g., 450
goal: approaches any g., 738; byproduct of g. setting, 727; commitment to a. . .g., 42; having no g. to reach, 723; is achieved, 728; of the corporation, 937; people who are really g. conscious, 32; self-interest in your g., 1155; should be just out of reach, 734
God: everything G. has made, 1362; gift from G., 1514; lets loose a thinker, 1572; offers to every mind,

1641; utterly abhors the boasts, 495
god: achieves the g., 726; become a g., 123; common g., 743; of every social system, 1732; playing the fool, 689
God's: presence in man, 336
gods: are on the side, 1515; very g. themselves, 857
going: concern stage, 500
gold: apples of g., 1722; is the wind, 956
golden: technique, 1296
good: at the beginning, 1359; bargain, 1143; believe g. of you, 1479; bigness is g., 1265; going g., 1217; entirely g., 413; example, 1165; how g. you are, 494; known much g., 1131; men, 1390; mental powers, 1664; never g., 800; news, 1619; no g. deed will go unpunished, 52; opinion, 1177; or bad, 1174; people, 1413; thing, 1340; very excellent g., 1361; what g. is it, 525; will, 1116; with hammers, 1286; words, 1726
goodness: is the only investment, 1659; piety and g., 630
goods: and services, 457; hand an accomplice the g., 1204; way of selling g., 1469
goose: plucking the g., 462
Gospels: scattered throughout the G., 600
gossip: unlike river water, 744
gossips: are not expected, 762
govern: for the many to g., 988; others, 365
government: by boobs, 686; every g. denounces it, 869
governments: people and g., 626
grain: which g. will grow, 1241
grandeur: is a dream, 1668
grandfathers: known to our g., 1357
grandparents: watching only the g., 466
grasp: within their g., 783
grave-making: sings at g., 1553
graveyards: are full, 964
gravity: emotional g. of the universe, 331; we can lick g., 191
great: adventure, 1411; discovery, 1192; harangue, 1706; man cannot be g., 665; man is only truly g., 67; men, 1695; power, 1268; task in life, 1383; things, 18; thinker, 1573;

I

M

motivation: employee m., 1394; provided with m., 1413
motive: mistakes in m., 1132
motives: were known, 1134
motor: man or a m., 1271
motorists: pioneering m., 276
motors: fly without m., 938
mountain: of problems, 1296; one side of a m., 812
mountaintop: falls down on the m., 984
mousetrap: better m., 1349
mousetraps: invent better m., 1245
mouth: keep your m. shut, 1483; keeps his m. shut, 256; open your m., 1704; shall show forth thy praise, 1389
mouths: they have m. but they speak not, 261
moves: that one can make, 1267
moving: keep m. or you fall down, 1344
mud: evolve out of the m., 1465; handful of m., 737
mugger: violent as a m., 872
multiplication: is vexation, 1506
multitude: [face] to the m., 811; opinion of the m., 1177; riches cover a m., 1671; wavering m., 756
mummy: walking m., 1566
muscle: risk m., 1420
music: we long to make m., 1719
muster: the basic soundness, 1381
mysticism: everything begins in m., 1162
mystique: building a m., 281

N

nail: see every problem as a n., 1286
name: better n., 1549; everyone gives, 617; for direction, 1250; no profit but the n., 270
names: badges and n., 180
natural: law: 47; order; 988; to humankind, 557
nature: calm and happy n., 772; ...comes up, 1349; crisis n., 1586; has not endowed us all, 9; human n., 1690; in n. there are no rewards, 441; inherent n., 978; men by n., 941; most feeble thing in n., 1560; of evil, 904; teaches beasts, 704
navel: gazing at one's n., 1554

near: slight not what's n., 735
necessary: every way n., 1656; more than is n., 1484; notes are often n., 1083; that which is n., 1139; word n., 1140
necessity: economic n., 215; impossibility yields to n., 1331; is the law, 1138; never made a good bargain, 1143; wrestles with n., 1141
neck: equipping us with a n., 1419
necktie: puts on a n., 1576
need: an M.B.A., 146; for approval, 504; for challenge, 1527; for managers, 364; more you n., 1500; sudden n., 1205; time of n., 1005; to see, 1308
needle: digging with a n., 1317
needless: innovations, 1348
neglect: of duty, 444; perpetual n., 1737
negotiate: for itself, 1599
neighbor: to annihilation, 309; what his n. says, 1150
neighbors: cause their n., 555
net: the biggest word, 1314
neurotic: and futile, 612
never: acquire a business, 949; an instant's truce, 1659; be disappointed, 1228; do merely one thing, 1306; dump a good idea, 1062; ever ever go see the boss, 1497; fails, 1659; find your delight, 1090; found again, 1596; get a two-minute warning, 1325; have your best trousers on, 1644; invest your money, 1316; just n. learn, 1702; known much good, 1131; let your mind get set, 1336; permanently withstand, 1276; put to sea, 1424; say more than is necessary, 1484; simple, 1614; surprised, 1690; take anything, 118; thank anybody, 1547; to return, 1595; underestimate the power, 1467
new: experience of the n., 205; find something new, 651; insights, 998; product, 1065; venture dream, 1332; venture life, 1457; ways to say no, 1013
newcomer: glad to see the n., 512
news: bearer of bad n., 263; bring back news, 800; diet of n., 749; get the n. right, 762; good n., 182, 1619
nickel: bet your last n., 219; five-cent n., 871

night: whole n., 1410
nights: left open to chance, 1256
noble: purpose, 1311; temptation, 1181; unquestionably n., 831
nobody: has a right, 1701; has to do anything, 1242; holds a good opinion, 486; speaks the truth, 1632
nobody's: business, 759
noise: a man or a motor makes, 1271; makes the most n., 291
non-conformists: were it not for the n., 318
none: but honest men, 795; knows the weight, 1415
nonheroic: anonymous and n., 1422
nonknowledge: ocean of n., 953
nonsense: anchor in n., 1559
nose: leading mankind by the n., 587
noses: of your friends, 668
nostalgia: is a seductive liar, 1024
notes: are often necessary, 1083; takes n., 994
nothing: absolutely in our power, 1263; a-year paid quarterly, 1319; but common sense, 1505; but concealment, 1618; can be done, 1060; can happen to you, 1444; cost more to do n., 1471; could discredit capitalism, 1669; designer term for n., 1402; ever happens, 1460; expects n., 1228; if not critical, 387; in life, 1436; inspires confidence, 1590; is easy, 1283; is ever accomplished, 38; is ever achieved, 1533; is good or bad, 1174; is impossible, 429; is more dangerous, 823; is more humiliating, 1042; is really frightening, 1427; is said nowadays, 656; is so good, 1360; is so simple, 1493; know absolutely n., 947; life grants n., 1741; now can stop it, 1629; real risk is doing n., 1431; satisfied with n., 1699; say absolutely n., 161; says n., 1480; so evil, 1102; so powerful, 826; so rivets the attention, 1354; telling you n., 1706; to say, 1481; ways to say n., 1080; when to say n., 1487; which men have less power over, 1703; worthwhile, 785
notice: obituary n., 1004
notions: preconceived n., 44
nuisance: a universal n., 140
number: of important operations,

1207; of people present, 1069
number-cruncher: image, 1446
numbers: come after the vision, 1328; expectations expressed in n., 154; greatest n., 66; make up their n., 1512; safety in n., 1430; shuffling the n., 967; work with n., 1504

O

obedience: blind o., 324; into duty, 1520
obey: safter to o. than to rule, 439
object: in every o., 864; of succeeding, 1336
objection: of atheists, 121
objectives: accepted o., 1258; know the o., 725; ultimate o., 1537
obligation: opportunity [implies] an o., 1408
oblivion: [ignorance] is o., 849
obscure: I become o., 249
observation: based on o., 1144; late and long o., 904; where o. is concerned, 1148
observe: a lot, 1149; the opportunity, 1147
obstacle: to discovery, 856
obstinate: virtue, 1665
obvious: spell out the o., 634
occasions: when it is...better, 1330
occupation: absence of o., 378; chief o. of mankind, 128
ocean: of nonknowledge, 953
oceans: swimming the o., 1158
offense: pardon one o., 443
offensive: war, 267
office: enters your o., 514; politics, 1160, 1163
old: American way, 1340; man, 1697; men, 1279
older: as I grow o., 1633; so much o., 1709
old-fashioned: way, 1324
old-style: companies, 1328
omelet: make an o., 1434
one-man: rule, 972
one-yard: line, 1325
open: mind, 1336; to chance, 1256
oneself: lies to o., 1029
operations: member of important o., 1207; plan for o., 157; serve the o., 989

religion: becomes a r., 1045
remedy: against this consumption, 362
remember: can anybody r., 1117; helping others to r., 1587; in order to r., 1030
remembering: as important as r., 892
remembrance: of prosperity, 1092
rendered: good by time, 1359
repentance: of a hypocrite, 813
report: annual r., 1400, 1401; memo or a r., 1079; understand the r., 1403
reports: annual r., 1399, 1402; becomes the end, 1398
repose: truth and r., 1641
reproach: hope to escape r., 1385
reputation: good r., 788; is an...imposition, 919
request: fair r., 518
requirements: of a job, 1734
research: market r., 652; statistical r., 1511; trouble with r., 1246; way we do r., 644
resign: isn't going to r., 521
resist: the temptation, 1636
resolution: thought and r., 1694
resource: strategic r., 937
resources: all r. are not obvious, 1387
respect: lose their r., 680
respectable: perfectly r., 603
respond: with a seminar, 1059
responsibilities: many r., 1410; part of his r., 433
responsibility: accept r., 428; building of r., 572; can never delegate r., 436; employees must be given r., 1413; escape all r., 167; facing r., 1411; fear of r., 1404; for achieving, 42; higher r., 1412; individual r., 1405; right implies a r., 1408
responsible: being r., 1395; to all men, 1407
result: desired r., 63; of thought, 1694; shot at without r., 1436
results: amazed at the r., 45; extraordinary r., 1067; nothing will get r., 1354; of his own example, 929
resume: best-looking r., 511; is a balance sheet, 99
retire: from the world, 765
retirement: on the job, 840
return: never to r., 1595; on invest-

ment, 1328
revenge: living well is the best r., 892; mild r., 909
reveries: secret r., 1274
reverse: suffer r., 1321
revolutionary: play the r., 321
reward: ample r., 1004; its own r., 1534; of entrepreneurial life, 1332; qualities, 1417
rewards: there are no r., 441
rhythms: tap crude r., 1719
rich: all the r. men, 1677; could hire other people, 1682; die r., 1679; dies r., 1681; get r. in business, 325; get r. with a pencil, 1379; ruleth over the poor, 1014; we could all be r., 1676; wishes to be r., 1680
riches: cover a multitude, 1671; have wings, 1668; thirst of r., 945; trusteth in his r., 1670
ride: in the direction, 1343
ridiculous: sublime and the r., 889
right: being in the r., 298; greatest r., 577; implies a responsibility, 1408, minority is always r., 1275; or wrong, 1167; questions, 1372; strength into r., 1520; the r., 1635; to censure, 768; to speak, 1701; to state unpopular views, 304; to tell people, 799; way, 1295; words, 1723
righteous: shall flourish, 1670; who believe, 232
rigor mortis: avoid organizational r.m., 206
risk: all things are at r., 1572; conquer without r., 1418; greater the r., 1421; his fortune, 1438; minimize or maximize r., 1432; muscle, 1420; never a r., 1139; of getting up in the morning, 1136; real r. is doing nothing, 1431
risk/return: game, 1432
risks: calculated r., 1425
risk-taker: man who is the real r., 1422
ritual: mumbo-jumbo r., 281
road: on the right r., 1237
roadblock: psychological r., 1202
robber: frightening as an armed r., 872
rock: find a r., 1552
roles: managerial r., 364
room: for dishonesty, 985; left alone in your r., 1607

Key Word Index

on our side, 1589; is short, 1740;
just doing t., 1129; lose a lot of t.,
1152; lost t., 1596; most of the t.,
1502; 93 percent of the t., 1512; of
great tragedy, 61; of need, 1005; of
old age, 1519; or place, 589; people
waste t., 1588; period of t., 1180;
rendered good by t., 1359; seeds of
t., 1241; settled by t., 613; spends all
his t., 1342; step at a t., 1335; takes
a long t., 616; tendency of our t.,
1678; that financial types, 1377;
thief of t., 1298; to do it right, 1213;
to reject it, 829; to relax, 1002; to
stop talking, 1480; to walk around
the job, 421; waste of t., 1079;
wasted t., 1594; wasting time: 1592;
we seldom have t., 1369; what t. it
is, 354; wise in t., 1684; wounds all
heels, 1582
times: happens enough t., 1087; rare
happiness of t., 771; trying t., 31;
were not hard, 1117
timing: strategy and t., 1474
tinkering: intelligent t., 1257
toads: mat of dead t., 1093
today: is safely past, 1236; is yesterday's pupil, 631; where I am t.,
1352
today's: complex company, 972
together: can decide, 1060; get it all
t., 359
toil: those that t., 627
tolerance: for indecision, 1377
tolerant: public is wonderfully t., 719
tomorrow: is not, 1236; may be trivial
t., 1557; yesterday not t., 1246
tone: and character, 257
tongue: fallen by the t., 761; have less
power over than the t., 1703; hold
his t., 694; proud t., 495
tool: it's just a t., 276; management
t., 516; prime t. for growing, 476;
public relations t., 1400
tools: effective t., 150
top: at the t., 1196; level consideration, 1231; management, 156; touch
at the t., 1542
torture: instrument of t., 153
touch: of the idealist, 731
tough: at the top, 1542; make it look
t., 281
tough-minded: ...manager, 1457
tower: ivory t., 1465

trade: and commerce, 595; for the
public good, 1131; ply their t., 440;
their daily t., 105
trademarks: crucial entrepreneurial t.,
547
tradition: authority and t., 1350; does
not mean, 996; imagination...frus-
trates t., 867
traditional: approach, 1244; organization chart, 1195
traffic: outside of t., 1064
tragedies: in life, 739
tragedy: of life, 723; time of great t.,
61
train: getting on a t., 1342
trains: run on time, 966
traitors: doubts are t., 313
traits: which favor that theory, 864
trance: hypnotic t., 678
transference: of feeling, 1459
traps: and pitfalls, 1455
treason: to civilization, 1556
tree: like a green bay t., 1268
trends: like horses, 1343
trick: of management, 978; of the
senses, 64
tricks: his tenures and his t., 960
trip: look forward to the t., 1551
triumph: without glory, 1418
trivial: may be t., 1557
trouble: borrow t., 1281; company's in
big t., 1401; financial t., 152; how
much t., 1150; looks for t., 1531;
meet t., 1205; of testing, 1610; when
they're in t., 1184; with most men,
993; with most of us, 31; with our
age, 722; with research, 1246; with
true humility, 491
troubled: seas, 1559
troublemaker: indicates a t., 1195
trousers: your best t., 1644
trout: in the milk, 907
truce: instant's t., 1659
true: becoming t., 1571; business
precept, 1164; clearly and undeniably t., 1608; definition of style,
1729; dreams come t., 1243; fears
this is t., 1187; friends are t., 1180;
...honesty is compatible, 790;
ideas that were t., 831; joy and
reward, 1332; know what is, 673;
leader, 975; obviously t., 164; opinions, 1176; the t., 1635; to ourselves,
343; to thine own self be t., 1012;

expands to fill the time, 1585; force
really wants, 983; getting w. done,
1125; goes to w., 1731; going to w.,
1341; hard w., 1741; has become a
leisure activity, 1006; hope and w.,
1234; I like w., 1738; importance of
the w., 1456; is hard, 1740; is the
grand cure, 1735; life's w., 1129;
make institutions w., 1422; makes
the approach w., 1381; managers at
w., 1586; need not be lost, 742;
part of any w., 1229; satisfying and
profitable w., 153; serious w., 1005;
tends to be watered down, 187; they
want things to w., 986; too senior
to w., 1072; turn $100 into $110 is
w., 1675; under those conditions,
1163; well done, 1309; will flow to,
14; willing to w., 844; with
numbers, 1504; with others, 1652;
worry kills more people than w.,
1744; worst w., 1130
workaholics: for w., 1451
working: go on w., 1142
workman: knows the w., 1358
workplace: progress in the w., 1450
works: that way in reality, 728
world: all over the w., 718; ambiguity
in the w., 374; arranging the w.,
284; as this w. goes, 789; business
w., 1049; chatter of the w., 760;
dishonesty...in their w., 985;
easiest job...in this w., 1327;
falsehoods in the w., 1023; fantasy
w., 1383; four friends in the w.,
747; genius appears in this w., 717;
greatest arts in the w., 660; half the
w. is composed, 241; in motion,
1098; in the business w., 628; in
this w., 1577; information in the w.,
877; is full of willing people, 844; is
given to lying, 1019; living in a w.,
880; managers in a w., 282; one
thing in the w., 763; perfection in
this w., 1616; place in the w., 1061;
retire from the w., 765; rich men in
the w., 1677; right in the w., 577;
slowest thing in the w., 782;
strongest man in the w., 1518; succeed in the w., 1530; things in the
w., 497; threaten the w., 1435; way
the w. is, 1377; will remember,
1216; would have known, 318
worlds: best of all possible w., 1187;

built new w., 1245; of thought, 1571
worm: catches the w., 1593
worriers: designated w., 1406
worry: kills more people, 1744; the interest paid, 1281
worse: and worse, 1222; bad and w.,
1223; sometimes much w., 1499;
than being talked about, 763; than
none, 1440; than you think, 1221;
the idea, 1421; the passage, 1439
worst: thing you can do, 1282; work,
1130
worth: little, 888; living, 1122, 1136;
more than a regiment, 820
worthless: goods are w., 1469
worthwhile: nothing w., 785
wound: what w. did ever heal, 784
wounded: walking w., 301
wrath: dragon and his w., 308; of
mediocrities, 1052
wretch: live like a w., 1679
wretched: souls, 1396
writer: memo w., 1076; protect the
w., 1081; resume w., 511
writing: a poem, 1743
written: in Chinese, 1416
wrong: always w., 1075, 1501; does
something w., 1489; forgetting of a
w., 909; I must be w., 93; most of
the time, 1502; research goes w.,
1511; right or w., 1167; right to be
w., 577

Y

yawn: killed by a y., 818
year: all the y., 1003; hanged in a y.,
1680; last y. alone, 1402
yearning: is...a good way to go
crazy, 843
years: employees spend y., 1463; I
spent, 1352; mature y., 1694; of
study and practice, 331; thousands
of y., 1158; through the y., 1146
yesterday: not tomorrow, 1246; was
the last day, 1617
yoke: of authority, 1350
young: men, 1279; men's minds, 1697;
pain, 1581; person, 1170
yourself: equal to y., 705
you see y., 342
youth: and age, 772; don't be afraid
of y., 981; in my y., 1192